DISCOMFORT
Earnest Whitley

A special thank you to Jameria for everything

"Mom, what are you doing?" I asked as I walked into her room. She's sitting in the middle of her floor, legs crossed, with cans and glass bottles surrounding her. I've never seen these types of bottles in her room before.

"I'm just relaxing, having a different type of juice." She motioned for me to sit by her. "Do you want some of this juice?"

"Is it good?" I excitedly asked as I sat down by her.

"Well, you're only six. I'm not sure if you'll consider this good or not. How about this, I'll let you try some. If you like it, you can always have some when you see me drinking it. And if you don't like it then you just don't like it."

"Deal!" I excitedly responded. She passed me an open bottle. The juice is blue and has HPNOTIQ on the front, whatever that spells. I smelled it. Well, it doesn't smell like the Kool-Aid I'm used to drinking. The bottle is pretty and again, the juice is blue, so it must be good. I raised the bottle up and took two swallows. Well, it's not Kool-Aid. It tastes like....I can't explain it. "I like it!" I shouted.

"Is that right?" Mom asked while smiling. I nodded my head. I took two more big swallows. I feel cool while drinking this.

"Where is Dad? Does Dad know we're drinking this?" Mom's face frowned.

"Dad just left two hours ago. I don't know if he's ever coming back." I now feel sad. What has happened to my dad?

"Why isn't he coming back?" I sadly asked. "Is he hurt?"

"No, nothing bad has happened to your dad. I'll say this, if he wants to come back, the door is always unlocked for him to do so. I'm not going to hold my breath."

"Why did he leave?" Mom shook her head.

"How about we talk about that later. With all this juice and soda around, I rather drink and not think about it. If you want, you're more than welcome to drink with me. If you feel like you've had enough juice, go back in your room and play with your toys. I'll be in here if you need me."

"Mom," I started, "I'm not going anywhere."

Chapter 1

Dear Diary,

Bottled up emotions can't be healthy. Keeping things internal without things being resolved can drive you crazy. I hate asking for help, so I try to figure things out myself, and just assume I'm always right. Does that really make me narcissistic? Maybe people are right. I still haven't.....processed my dad cheating on my wonderful mom while I was a kid. It would have hurt if it was with another woman, but for it to be with another man? Mom just flat out told me, no sugarcoating it. How in the hell am I supposed to process that information as a kid? How am I supposed to process that as an adult? Since I was six, Mom and I have been drinking beer and liquor together, numbing the pain. Never discussing the matter, just drinking in silence. You can always feel her sadness in the air. When I was ten is when the memory loss started to occur. That's when the drinking habits really formed. Before that I was maybe having two cups a week. When I turned ten it turned into a daily occurrence. Beer after beer, hour after hour. I'd blackout, wake up crying because I have a massive headache, let the headache leave, then start back drinking. Wow, I've been an alcoholic since I was ten. How did I make it through school? Most of elementary, junior high, and high school is a blur. I only remember certain scenes. Some type of way I made friends, though I can't recall the scenes of meeting most of them. I remember a teacher telling me that I'm very quiet. No teacher, I'm not quiet, I'm drunk. Why can't I have this talk with a psychiatrist? Because I feel like a psychiatrist is going to internally judge me though it's their job not to. I'm admitting to myself that I need help. Or I can just pick up another beer. I don't even drink to get a buzz anymore. I think I'm permanently numb. The only time the numbness is gone is when I'm in love. Love makes me put the beer down, makes me live in the moment. It's more about caring for the other person, and less about me receiving love. Loving someone makes me forget about myself, and I truly enjoy it. I love giving someone else my attention. And that leads me to now. I think I'm in love but have a beer in my other hand as I write this. Then I'll go to work and go through my shift, probably having two more beers throughout the shift. It's funny, I have true feelings that I should be writing down right now, but sometimes I'm even scared to see my own thoughts on paper.

Marcus

Today is 'family day.' All the family is getting together at my cousin's home. He invited my girlfriend of four years, Tiffany, but she is at work. I would prefer her to be with me. She has the charm in the relationship. The family loves her and wants me to marry her. How can I marry someone that doesn't really know me? I've hidden my alcoholic tendencies the entire time of us being together. Does that mean our entire relationship is a lie? I guess it's easier to hide since we don't officially live together. We sleep at each other's homes a few days out the week. When I'm with her, I don't want any liquor. If that's the case, then I guess the logical idea would be to permanently move in together and maybe forget about the liquor? I guess this is my way of admitting that I love liquor more than her. What a horrible thing to admit to myself. Do I blame her? Or am I just that good at hiding my problem? Or does love really blind you from a lot of flaws? What flaws of hers are love blinding me from? I should have brought a beer with me, though there should be plenty of beer and liquor at my cousin's house. I'm more of a lonely drinker, unless it's with my mom. You'll never see me at the bar drinking. I even tell people I'm not a drinker. I wonder can people tell that I'm lying just by looking at me. Maybe everyone sees through my words and it only makes sense in my head.

Everyone is at my cousin's home, and I mean everyone. People I've never seen before are here. I thought this was going to be more of a family gathering. I'm wrong, this is more like a party. With him having a two-story home with a pool in his backyard, he has enough space. Everyone is standing around, socializing while the music is playing loudly, of course while drinking. I'm doing the same, but have a cup of orange juice. Someone must be the responsible adult around here.

"Marcus, you're not having any liquor?" It's my cousin Misha and a beautiful light brown skinned woman. I'm trying hard not to stare at her. I've never cheated on Tiffany before (liquor doesn't count) and I don't plan on starting now. I have female friends I communicate with sometimes, but it's nothing more than communication. Plus, Tiffany knows about them all. Her skin color reminds me of Halle Berry. The braids in her hair are neatly done. None of her body assets are too small or too big. Everything fits her small frame perfectly.

"How do you know I have no liquor in my cup?" I asked while looking down at my clear cup.

"Because it looks like a normal orange. I can tell there's nothing mixed with that orange juice." I smiled and looked away. "It may be sad that I can notice these type of things, but what can I say? I'm a professional drinker." My whole family may be alcoholics. "This is my friend, Camille."

"Hi Camille, I'm Marcus." I extended my hand to shake hers. Misha's phone rang. She answered the phone and quickly walked away. Now Camille and I stand in the kitchen, alone. I just noticed that no one else is in here. Everyone's in the backyard. Now there is silence and I feel the awkwardness coming. "So, how long have you known Misha?"

"You must have felt the awkward vibe," she said with a smile. I smiled and took a sip of my orange juice. It's hard to figure out how to go about this conversation because.... I'm definitely thinking about this too hard.

"So, why didn't you bring your boyfriend with you?" I asked. "Or is he in the backyard watching us from afar?" She laughed.

"I didn't bring him because he doesn't exist. Where's your girlfriend?"

"She's at work. I didn't feel like this was important enough for her to miss work over. Why no boyfriend?"

"Let's just say I'm a complicated person to deal with."

"I'm listening."

"I have a unique personality. I'm into different things. I can come off as intimidating. My emotional flaws are a lot to deal with. I have some unresolved internal issues."

"Don't we all," I said. I'm not sure if I meant that as a question or a statement.

"Well, tell me a flaw of yours," she said in a seductive tone. Her voice is sexy. I feel her energy pulling me in. I have enough female friends, I don't need another. It's something about her.

"You're not ready for my flaws," I truthfully said.

"Why do you say that?"

"Because I use my flaws to scare people away, and if you happen to stay around, I have a habit of thinking that means you're meant to be in my life. See, I just told you a flaw without intending to."

"I have daddy issues," she blurted out.

"So do I. I hate my dad with a strong passion. I will never stop hating him."

"May I ask why?"

"How about you tell me about your daddy issues first."

"How about you give me your number, and if you're free from your girlfriend when I text you, we can continue this conversation." She pulled out her phone and handed it to me. So much for me feeling like I don't need any more friends.

I enjoyed this party. Everyone seemed to have a good time. Even my mom, who was beyond drunk, seemed to have a good time. I've been expecting her to randomly breakdown and start crying in front of everyone, while telling EVERYTHING when she's drunk. It hasn't happened. Mom isn't sad while drunk. She's quite happy while drinking, except when it's just the two of us. I don't think she's told anyone why my dad and her split, not even my grandmother. It's our little secret, and I plan to forever keep it that way. It shouldn't be legal to have as much hate as I have for my dad.

FOUR MONTHS LATER

"This is the first time we've met at a restaurant." I sat down. She looks beautiful as always. "Now that I think about it, we've never been around a lot of people before. When we met doesn't count. Thank you for having respect for my relationship, or what little is left of it. My feelings for her are dying. You said we needed to talk. Please don't tell me you're pregnant." I smiled and gently reached and touched her hand.

"I was born a male," she calmly stated. My body has gone numb. Her hand was just warm, now it feels like I'm holding air. My mind is trying to process her words. Maybe I heard her wrong. I'm pretty sure I'm displaying a blank expression. "Marcus, did you hear me?" My mouth wants to open but can't seem to. "Marcus, answer me."

"Huh?"

"Did you hear me?"

"I'm…. I'm not sure."

"I was born a male." Yes, the words I heard were correct. "Well, kind of."

"How? How is that possible?" I asked. "I've seen you naked. You have a vagina. I've been inside of that vagina with NO CONDOM!" Heads have turned towards us.

"Lower your voice," she whispered. The shock and fear are kicking in at the same time. I feel myself losing breath. Is this it? Is this how I die? I never imagined it happening this way. So many thoughts are racing through my mind. My body is starting to uncontrollably shake. I think…. I think……

"MARCUS!" I opened my eyes. I see a ceiling. Where am I? My back hurts. I can feel that I'm lying on a hard floor. People are surrounding me now. What happened? Why am I lying on this hard floor? "Marcus, you're alive!" It's Camille's voice. "CPR really does work." I now remember what happened. Well, I remember the conversation. I'm still in a daze.

"Are you okay?" A man's voice asked.

"Baby, are you okay?" Camille asked. I honestly wish I would have stayed unconscious. I don't want to process everything. Maybe I heard her wrong, though I'm almost sure she repeated herself.

"I'm fine," I said as I got up. I see that I'm still in the restaurant.

"Baby, you fainted." Hearing her say "baby" now gives me the chills. What am I supposed to do now? I was contemplating leaving Tiffany. I don't love her anymore, and she's done nothing to deserve losing my love. Now I'm in love with.... a man? How is this even possible? I need clarity, and need it fast.

The car ride has been silent. Camille hasn't even faced me. Her face has stayed staring out the window. Who's going to break the silence first? I feel that she should. She's the one with the explaining to do.

"So, you're not going to speak?" I asked.

"The last time I spoke you ended up having a panic attack. That's the last thing I need to happen while you're driving. I'm not ready to die." I would usually smile at a comment like that. This isn't a smiling matter. I pulled up to her apartment.

"Soooo?"

"Marcus, what do you want me to say?" I must stay calm. I almost called her a bitch. I need a drink. I need more than a drink. Give me beer and vodka combined. I just want to blackout. How could she ask me such a question? And I must stop saying 'she.' Am I supposed to refer to Camille as 'it?' I feel a headache coming.

"Everything, Camille," I calmly stated. "Tell me everything."

"I don't know what else to say."

"You seemed like you had a lot to say at the restaurant!"

"We were surrounded by people. I felt safe."

"Are you saying that I'm crazy?" I angrily asked.

"Going by your tone, you possibly may be?"

"YOU'RE A MAN," I screamed. "Oh my God, it's sinking in. I've slept with a man. I'm officially homosexual. I feel myself getting weak."

"Marcus, I'm not a man anymore." Camille gently touched my hand. I quickly slapped it away.

"Don't touch me!" I feel myself starting to sweat. I'm breathing hard. I don't like how my body is feeling at the moment. I need a drink. I need a drink while sitting with my mom to make the thoughts go away. I've cheated on Tiffany. I've lied to Tiffany. I've damaged Tiffany mentally, emotionally, spiritually, though she doesn't know yet, with a man. It now makes sense, the conversation we had when I first met her, when she said she's a complicated person.

"Marcus, may I explain myself?" My breathing is calming down. Why is her voice so…… soothing? She's not even a woman. How is this possible? The whole situation. "I'm a transgender," she started, "I have the hormones, body parts, and emotions of a woman."

"Please, get out." I unlocked the doors.

"I'm not finished. When I was five my father told my mother she'll never be a good enough woman to make him happy. Since he impregnated a "whore, a horrible soul, and horrible woman as a human being" and made me, I'd attract the same type of girls and women for my entire life. From that day forth he referred to my mother as a "bitch." The weird part is that she answered to it like she was some type of slave. He started to beat on her while in front of me. My mother seemed like such a beautiful soul. Why was she taking so much abuse? Something made me want to be my mother, at least the version I viewed her as."

"After every ass whipping from him she would come hug me, even while bloodied. She continued to love him, every day, even still today. My father's words stayed in my head. All I seemed to attract were horrible girls and women. Or maybe it was me being unhappy in my heart, and fucked up in the head. Sex with women was never pleasurable. I'd never release while inside of a woman. Every woman's sex couldn't be bad. So, I started telling myself it was me. Then I kept in my mind that I wanted to be my version of my mother. That thought kept replaying in my mind."

"To make things worse, since the eighth grade I was known as the boy with the horrible sex throughout the whole school. All the girls used to laugh at me once the word spread. I think they used to have sex with me just to see if I was really bad. I guess I was really bad in the bed. I don't know if it was because my stroke game was really that horrible, or I was just damaged in the head. All the horrible events replayed in my head while having sex. Two years after I graduated high school I was done. I was done being ridiculed by girls and boys, men and women. So, I went all in. I told myself God had made a mistake with me. There's no reason a person should go through so much hurt and confusion from such an early age."

"So, I went from Cornell to Camille, literally. I wrote my mother a letter before I did it, telling her I'm moving to another country and not to look for me. I only know they're still together because I went to the grocery store they've been going to for years. They didn't notice the new me. After the process was complete I started having sex with men. It was the first time I ever came. I got to feel what it was like to be on the other side, to receive the pressure."

"The same scenes from when I was five came into my head, but for whatever reason it didn't matter while having sex as a woman. The thoughts eventually went away. I think I became addicted to the cuddling process after sex. The being held, feeling like everything is going to be alright."

"Wow."

"Wow?" she repeated. "I just poured my life story out to you. Is that all you have to say? Wow, that's it?"

"Do you really expect me to know what to say at this very moment? Do you realize what news you've dropped on me? Like, why would you even tell me? How would I've ever known?"

"The feelings are growing, I can feel it. How could I not tell you?" I pointed for her to get out. "Marcus, are you really going to avoid having this conversation with me?" I turned on the engine to the car. I hope that gives her the answer she's looking for. She opened the door, got out, and slammed it. What just happened?

Chapter 2

Dear Diary,

Do you remember when I told you I'm scared to see some of my thoughts on paper? OK, here are those thoughts. Here is the real me. Absolutely no one knows these thoughts, not even my mom. I'm very afraid of relationships. Connection scares me, it's actually one of my biggest fears. I witnessed something as a kid with one of my mom's very rare drunk friends that has forever put a scar on my heart. No, there was nothing physically done to me, but seeing what I saw at an early age changed my outlook on life. It made me believe that nothing lasts long, nothing is worth holding on to. I have a horrible memory, but this is one memory that has stuck with me. I thought I was ready to put the scene on paper but now see that I'm not. These past four years of my relationship has been an internal battle of me accepting that I may have something real, but then remembering that nothing lasts long. I've tried overriding these thoughts with some version of love, but admit to myself I don't know how to love. Honestly, what am I doing with my life right now? Another question I don't have the answer to, which seems to be the theme of my life.

Marcus

These are the moments that can't be matched, Tiffany and I going on our Barnes and Noble date. This is where we met. Since meeting, we agreed to come here twice a month, block out the rest of the world and just talk about books. I've never met a woman more passionate about books. How people talk about movies and TV shows, how I talk about sports, is how Tiffany talks about books. I like to read, but she loves to read. There's definitely a difference. Just one of the many reasons I fell for Tiffany. She's the opposite of almost any woman I've met. She doesn't entertain gossip. The only TV she watches is the news, which I hate because all the news seems to do is depress me. She loves creating and loves to stay busy. She's either writing a book, painting a picture, or trying to learn a new skill. The icing on the cake is her conversation skills. We've never become stuck with no new topics to discuss. Tiffany ALWAYS has something with substance to talk about. She makes me learn without forcing it. If she brings up a topic I don't know of, I'll go learn about it and bring the topic back up on another day.

No, she's not perfect. She has her flaws. Her sex drive isn't as high as mine, mainly because she's always tired at the end of the day from working and learning. She does take random days off and invite me over for a day of sex, or will randomly order a nice suite and already be naked when I arrive. Another flaw is she's a health freak. I guess that would be a great thing for most men, but when you're hiding your alccholism, it's a horrible thing. She begs me to go get a check-up with her. I always find an excuse, even if it's creating a mild argument. I've been drinking since I was six, I can't imagine what my liver looks like. I'm not getting sick, or anything of that nature, so I'll pass on the check-ups.

"Marcus, what's your favorite book?" she asked.

"We've been dating for years and you don't know my favorite book? How dare you?" She burst out laughing. "I know your favorite book."

"What's my favorite book?" she asked. I looked away. "Look at you! You don't even know my favorite book. You should be ashamed of yourself. How many Barnes and Noble dates have we been on?"

"Your favorite book is 'The 5 Languages Of Love,' by Gary Chapman. Now take that." She smiled and took a sip of her coffee.

"And your favorite book is 'Lying' by Sam Harris. Now you take that." I laughed and looked away. I would be lowkey upset if she didn't know my favorite book. Books is what brought us together. This is our place to be to get away from the world. This is where I need to be to get away from my current reality. I'm also trying to stop drinking. I'll use the bookstore as a distraction.

"Do you ever think about if we were moments late?" I asked. "What if I'd came to Barnes and Noble an hour earlier or later and you not have been here? Maybe we wouldn't be together today. It's amazing how each moment in life counts."

"And if it was possible, I'd spend every moment with you." She kissed me on the lips. "Except when I need my alone time. I may enjoy those moments better than you," she smiled. Half of my mind is in the moment; the other half is being in a mixture of emotions. I haven't even begun to process what happened the other day. I don't want to believe it. I really don't want to think about it. Camille has been calling, but it's hard to answer when you don't know what to say.

"Marcus, are you lost in your thoughts?" Tiffany asked. *Well, not anymore.* How long was I silent? I don't even remember the question I asked. Did I even ask a question? My memory is horrible. "You don't have to answer. I notice when you go deep into thought."

"You may know me better than I know myself if that's the case." She smiled and gave me a wink. If she really knew me she would probably kill me. Ok, maybe killing me is a bit extreme. She'd definitely leave with no hesitation, and I don't think I would stop her.

"Are you aware of all your flaws?" Tiffany asked.

"That's an odd question. I like to think I'm in tune with myself. Please enlighten me if I'm not."

"There's a layer of emotion and passion that you lack. I'm not sure if you purposely don't display it, or if it's really not there. I notice the same thing with your mom, which had me thinking it may be genetic. No, I'm not asking you to change your ways for me. I accept you for you. It's just something I've noticed." I stood up and started towards the bookstore's entrance. I don't know how to respond to her interpretation. I'm going to eventually have to answer her question. Luckily, later is better than now.

We're riding in silence, not even the music is playing. There's a weird vibe in the air. It's not an air of tension, but an air of confusion. Maybe the confusion is on my part. Of course I'm confused. I pulled up to Tiffany's apartment. Some sex would be good right now, but suddenly I have a guilty conscience. I probably wouldn't get an erection. She kissed me and got out. I need a drink. Let me get home before I make another unwise decision.

Dear Diary,

Initial thought, initial emotion, initial reaction. I was reading something that says those three traits are truly a person's make up. My initial thought, I miss Camille. My initial emotion, I'm very confused. My initial reaction is to forgive. What type of person does this make me? I don't know the answer and it's hurting my heart. I don't want to think about it all. I really want to drink my problems away. Thinking, in itself, has to be a curse. Something may be wired wrong in my brain. I have the ability to think myself into insanity, but won't stop it. How can I stop it? I can change my thoughts, try to think of something more positive. How do you do that when the person responsible for ninety percent of your positivity is the person you're doing wrong? So that would mean I'm still thinking on a negative frequency, right? Am I crazy? No, I'm not crazy. I'm just having a series of actions that's causing worse actions. So, I need to change my actions, but what if my heart doesn't want to? Am I supposed to fight what the heart wants? Isn't that the true definition of self-torture? But the heart has the ability to be wrong, correct? Yes, that's what I have to repeat to myself. The heart has the ability to be wrong. REPEAT, the heart has the ability to be wrong.

Marcus

"Marcus, I've missed you." Camille leaned to hug me.

"That's nice to know." I said as I avoided her hug. Why did I decide to meet her at Starbucks? I have no clue. What am I doing here? I have the answers, but am not ready to admit them to myself.

"I'm not good enough for a hug anymore?" she asked. I sat down and took a sip of my coffee. "Is this going to be an awkward situation?" she asked as she sat down.

"What would be your definition of things being normal?"

"Um, for things to continue to go in the direction they were going? Is that asking for too much? Are you going to sit here and act like you don't have feelings for me anymore? What, they erased in a week? Your heart is built differently? Feelings don't die quickly when they're real. Tell me I'm wrong."

"You're wrong," I bluntly replied. "I had feelings for who I thought you were. There's a difference. There's a big difference." I thought something was different while having sex with her. I let the passion override my thinking. 'Shallow' would be the best word to describe the sex. I'm thinking too much, I must focus.

"And who do you think I am now?"

"It doesn't matter. What I should be asking is why would you want things to keep going in the same direction? I have a significant other. That makes me a cheater. So, you don't mind being with a cheater? What makes you think I wouldn't do you in the same manner? Or you don't care? Or you are what you decide to sleep with?" She took a sip of her coffee.

"If this is your way of trying to guilt yourself out of this situation, out of these feelings, then you're making a horrible attempt."

"Or are you avoiding the obvious?" Her eyes widened. I usually love the vibe of Starbucks. The vibe isn't the same today. We should have chosen another place to meet at. Great, now every time I come to Starbucks alone or with Tiffany I'm going to think about this day. Maybe I'll stop coming to Starbucks altogether.

"Marcus, what's the obvious? Please let me know."

"The obvious is....the obvious is this, us, was a big mistake. Mistakes happen, let's just move on."

"What if it was love at first sight between the two of us? You can't deny the fact we connected easily and quickly. I know you don't experience this with everyone." I took a deep breath.

"Love at first sight between two people is just two emotionally damaged people making a connection. And I don't think I'm emotionally damaged, so that's not what it was with us."

"If you're not emotionally damaged then what are you?" I quickly stood up.

"I'm a person who steered off track momentarily. You made me aware of my wrong steering. I'm back on track and must thank you for that. I'm not sure what I expected to get out of this, but just want to tell you we're done. It was just a phase in our life. They say there's a lesson in every situation. I hope you understood the lesson with us."

"You never answered my question. Who do you think I am now?" I turned around and walked away. I have to get my life back in order, if that's possible. If I forgive myself for my actions and vow to myself to be faithful from now on, would that be enough? Would that override not telling Tiffany what I did? Or do I know deep down inside I'm lying to myself? One day I'm going to officially lose my mind.

****

"Do you think people are whores because they want to be?" Tiffany asked. Why does this question come to her mind while we're outside looking at the stars? I'll never understand. Tiffany's thoughts are everywhere.

"If you were whoring, why do you think you would be doing it?" I asked. Tiffany seems to be in deep thought. I wonder how many men Tiffany has slept with. I've never asked because I learned not to ask questions I really don't want to know the answer to. She's never asked my amount of bodies either. I only have six under my belt, for better or worse.

"I think I'd be doing it if I was trying to fill some type of emotional void. I think I would use sex as a drug since drugs really scare me. I would move from body to body, in hope of not thinking about someone or something. It seems weird to think like that, I guess for the simple fact I've never done it before. Sex is powerful, I think it would be used as a memory blocker."

"So, that's why you have sex with me?" I jokingly asked. She punched me in the shoulder.

"Well, you're the only person I've had sex with in years, and hope you're the last person. Hypothetically speaking, you cheating on me could turn me into a whore." *Marcus, stay calm.* "I would sleep around, not being able to process your reasoning for cheating on me. I could be wrong, but I honestly don't think I deserve that."

"I don't see why I'd ever cheat on you."

"I know me pretty well. I would try to block out that memory. It would be hard for me to understand, and that may cause me to go crazy. I would first try to use painting to fill that void, but would probably only come away with depressing pictures. I haven't been through an extremely miserable situation in a long time. I've always had you here to help me through them before the situation became too extreme. How would I go about having my backbone be the exact thing he helps me with? Which is all of my problems."

"Wow."

"It would be tough on my part. I know it would. You've protected me a lot. I'm not saying I need you, but God knows I really enjoy having you in my life. You make my life easier. If I had to handle everything on my own, I'd go crazy. I'm very thankful for having you in my life. Now, I say all that for you to end up cheating on me?"

"You becoming a whore would definitely be understandable," I laughed.

"Marcus, I love you."

"I love you too." I need a drink ASAP. ASAP isn't soon enough to describe how quickly I need a drink. My heart is beating fast. Tiffany has just revealed the damage I've done to her without her knowing. I never realized the cause and effect concept in life until now.

Tiffany is sleep and I'm off to the liquor store. I should be in the bed next to her, holding her, but need to clear my mind. I need to flush the thoughts away, even if it's just for a moment. Tiffany is going to be upset when she wakes up and see I'm not there. She has every right to be, but doesn't know about my habit so she won't understand. I'll figure out an excuse, even if it's a bad one. I need to be at my own place, away from everyone.

Great, Tiffany is calling me. How is that possible? Why did she wake up so quickly? Did she not feel me next to her while sleeping? I have to turn around and go back now. Why is she ruining my escape? I need an excuse. I'll say I got hungry and wanted to get chips and cookies. I don't have chips and cookies but will say I didn't reach the store because I saw her phone call. Why can't things go my way? Back to Tiffany's apartment I go.

I opened my eyes. I feel the sun beaming from the window. I should go back to sleep and start over. I feel annoyed and aggravated. I'm upset about last night, I wanted liquor. I needed liquor and still need liquor. I need to get away from here, but now must act like everything is fine. My excuse last night worked. Tiffany knows I have a bad habit of eating at night, and she hates it. She argues that I don't need those extra calories at night and I take my fast metabolism for granted. She feels that one day I will wake up forty pounds heavier and then get mad at the world. She has a point, though I won't admit it.

Camille has been on my mind. I'm constantly trying to fight off the thoughts. The thoughts of….everything, the entire situation. I try to indulge in things that will help me not think about it, though nothing seems to work. I don't want to think about it, thinking doesn't change anything. My own thoughts sometimes scare me so I try to suppress them. My mind is telling me to go to work to pick up this extra shift, since Tiffany is at work. My heart is telling me to go see Camille. *The heart has the ability to be wrong.*

"What are you doing here?" Camille asked as she opened the door. Yes, I listened to my heart. I'm now realizing that not only does the heart have the ability to be wrong, but the heart also has no logic. I can't stay away from her, even though I know I should. I should walk away now and get back into my car. All logic points to me not being here, and yet, here I stand.

"Camille, I've missed you." Her face has softened. She wants to fight it, which she should. She should fight the urges for the both of us. She should close the door and go about her day. When I continue to knock, put on her headphones and ignore me. Someone has to be the strong person in this situation. "You're all I've been thinking about."

"You said I was emotionally damaged. Those words stuck with me. You should give me space while I figure out how to emotionally repair myself. You may actually be right about me being damaged, though you're the last person I wanted to hear that from." I see she's not going to let me come into her place. I should erase that idea from my thoughts.

"Camille, I made a mistake. I was wrong."

"So, you're saying I'm not emotionally damaged? And don't lie to me. You've blatantly admitted you're a liar. You've admitted in a way that most people wouldn't admit it, especially to people they care about. Marcus, all your words stung. Each word stayed with me. I dissected each sentence when I sat down after our conversation. I convinced myself that you're right."

"Camille, I was wrong."

"Then why would you say such harsh words? Do you not stop to think about my sensitivities as a woman?" I have a bunch of scattered thoughts in my head. I'm trying to put them in order but am not having luck. I don't know how to explain myself at the moment. All I can do is stare at her. The structure of her face is beautiful. I really wish we could move past this and take our feelings out on each other in the bedroom. Yes, I think I would be able to express my feelings much better in the bedroom. "Marcus, are you going to say anything?"

"Camille, you ever had a bunch of thoughts in your head but didn't know how to express them correctly?"

"No," she meanly replied. "I've learned that's an excuse we give ourselves when we either really don't want to say what we're thinking, or we don't want to sort out the thoughts. So, I'll never use that excuse. I'd just come to the conclusion that I don't really want to tell you what I'm thinking, and I'd have to accept that decision." She shut the door. Wow, she really didn't let me come in. This is not how I pictured it in my head. My heart aches.

"Camille," I mildly shouted as I knocked on the door. I don't want to raise my voice too loud. The sun hasn't fully risen, her neighbors may still be sleep. What am I doing here? My life is in shambles at the moment. There's only one way for me to try to figure it out. That's the way I always do, by talking to myself and seeing what I learn.

Dear Diary,

When things get chaotic is when I try to have outer body experiences. I try to step out of my body and look at the situation. I have feelings for Camille, that's undeniable. I want to step back and look at my feelings and situation with Tiffany. Tiffany says there's a layer of emotion and passion that I lack with her. I really didn't realize it until she said it, but will admit that it is true. It left when my dad left us, and I don't know how to get it back. I think I move through life expecting to get hurt. I don't want to, but know I have a permanent scar on my heart, so it's become a foregone conclusion that I will be hurt. I didn't realize it, but I accidently act that way towards Tiffany. Tiffany has done nothing wrong our entire relationship. Well, nothing wrong that would cause any major problems, and I can't seem to open that next layer of love, which she probably deserves. It's been four years and counting. I shouldn't say 'probably' because she does deserve it. Something inside of me won't allow it. Do I trust her? Yes, I trust her a lot. I don't think she'd do anything to harm my life. But, and there's always a but, I never thought my dad would do anything to hurt me, and he left. So, I guess I always try to expect the unexpected. Fast forward to Camille. It could be viewed that I'm more passionate with her than Tiffany. Why is that? I've been with Tiffany four years and counting. I've known Camille four months, maybe five. How is there more passion, thoughts, love, with essentially a stranger? What if I did leave Tiffany for Camille. Would my same habits just transfer over? Would I be as guarded? Would Camille accept my alcoholism? Maybe she will because we're still new. I know Tiffany won't, and she shouldn't. I wait four years to tell her I have a drinking problem? Yeah, that won't work. But I have a lot of problems I won't express to her. Does that mean we're really in love? I won't express my true feelings to anyone, so does that mean I'm incapable of being in love with anyone? Just some random thoughts.

Marcus

    I turn into another person when I write in my diary. It's like someone takes over me and I'm able to express my thoughts easily. Maybe it's something about writing thoughts down that I enjoy. Some of my entries sometimes scare me. With some entries I convince myself it wasn't me that wrote them, and I actually see my handwritten sentences.

    Now that I've completed some writing, I can now have a drink. I remembered a spare bottle of liquor I keep stashed. I'm not an alcoholic, I got the idea from a movie. A nice bottle of Hennessy, my mom's favorite liquor. Whenever I'm feeling down, this is my choice of liquor. When I'm not feeling down, this is still my first choice of liquor. Ok, I really am an alcoholic. There's nothing wrong with that.

    Five swallows in and I now feel great. I can't remember the last time I had a drink so this feels lovely. I feel calm and all my problems have seemed to go away. Nothing else matters. It's just me and the little world of my own that I'm in. I wish I could permanently feel this way. I want the permanent numbness. Feeling no pain for the rest of my life would be great. Is it possible? Maybe I'll sit here for a few hours and try to figure it out.

    Is there something wrong with a person who has no problem drinking alone? I have a horrible memory, but I remember the first time I had liquor by myself. It was on a night I was missing my dad and Mom was gone. I was eight years old and didn't know how to deal with my loneliness. Sixteen years later and I still don't know how to deal with it, but that's not the point. I don't remember my thought process during that night, I just remember no longer feeling sad. I wasn't happy, but I wasn't sad. I wish I could go back to those moments. Not that I would change anything, but just to be a kid again would be great.

The bottle of Hennessy is completed. I now want to meditate, which I try to do three days a week. I've never tried to meditate while drunk, I wonder what that feels like. Tiffany got me into meditation. Most people would say Tiffany has changed me for the better. That's on the outside looking in. I guess in reality I haven't changed at all. I'll just sit here and look at the ceiling.

****

"Mom, how do you go about resolving unresolved issues?" Mom and I aren't drinking, just spending quality time together. I need for someone to record our conversations while drunk and sober. I want to see the difference. I want to see how our conversations flow.

"That's a great question," Mom replied. "I usually try not to think about them, hoping that they'll go away. No, that way usually doesn't work, but it's always my first resort. My second resort is by asking strangers for advice. You may wonder why I would ask a stranger. My logic is I'd expect a stranger to judge me. It's when family judges me that hurts the most, which is why I don't talk to them about my problems, even the smallest. You'd be surprised at some of the good advice a stranger will give you."

"Has the first way ever worked? Has any problem ever went away from not thinking about it? I hope the answer is yes. If so, I'll practice the first way more often." Mom has a look of concern on her face. I think I've said too much.

"What's going on that you haven't talked to me about?" Yes, I've said too much, great. "And the answer to your question is yes, but also no. The problems I've wanted to go away never did. They'd stay there, lingering around until I found a way to solve them. That process usually sucks because I have a hard time coming up with solutions to problems on my own. I really suck at it. It makes me feel like I'll always be dependent on someone, like I can't handle life on my own."

"Mom," I started, "There's nothing wrong with needing help in life. We all need a shoulder to lean on sometimes. I don't think life is meant to solve by yourself." Mom sighed and looked at the floor. If I know her like I think I do, she's probably wishing she had a drink right now. I say that because that's exactly what I'd be thinking if I was her right now, and we tend to think alike.

"The world is too judgmental to ask for help. Nothing seems genuine anymore. Everyone seems to have an ulterior motive these days. Why can't you do something because it's the right thing to do? That seems like a lot to ask for today. I rather suffer by myself. That's not saying I'm not open to letting people into my life. I'm just not disappointed in the result anymore. It used to bother me, now I just look at it as a big part of life."

"Well, Mom, you'll always have me. Fuck everyone else. Loyal is the only way I know how to be." Mom nodded her head in agreement. Did I just lie to my mom? I'm kind of being loyal to two people who want the same thing from me. Does that make me the definition of unloyalty? No, that just makes me….confused. Here I go, thinking myself into wondering is something wrong with me. "Mom, I'm going to leave now."

"When are you going to bring Tiffany over to see me? I really like her. I think without her you'd be an emotional wreck. I know loyalty when I see it because it's something I fiend for. Don't you ever do her wrong. Good women are hard to find today. It's hard to find that person who is spiritually compatible.

"Spiritually compatible," I started, "I don't think I've ever heard that term before."

"It's easy to find someone you're sexually compatible with. Shit, that could be multiple people, but to find that spiritual connection, it's very rare. I feel that's what you and Tiffany have. I like her and want to be a grandmother one day. Don't mess up something good." I nodded my head. Nodding my head is the only thing I can do. I could mention Camille, but Mom just gave me her answer. I can't take it anymore, I'm going to do what I should have done months ago.

"Do you love yourself?"

"You're the therapist. I'm paying you for answers. How about you tell me." I'm laid on the therapist's couch, looking at the ceiling. I refuse to talk while looking the therapist in the eye. Something about eye contact with him bothers me.

"How can I tell you about how you feel on the inside?" His question stings. I know it's a logical question, and I should have a logical answer, but I don't have a logical answer about anything. Well, I take that back. All my logical answers seem to be wrong, which is why I'm here.

"Of course, I love myself. Love just doesn't seem to love me back."

"Why do you think that?"

"Love doesn't love anyone."

"What is your definition of love?" Another question that stings. I have no answer. How do I explain love? I don't know. A strong feeling?

"How do you expect me to give a definition to such a strong feeling? Is that even possible?"

"Maybe so you can have a sense of what it is you're feeling and why you're feeling it?" Why did I come here? I feel my head about to explode. I want to scream "I DON'T KNOW. I DON'T KNOW ANYTHING!!!" The thoughts that run through my head.

"I want my thoughts sorted out," I blurted.

"Excuse me?"

"Do you ever sit or lay on this couch, in the same position I'm in now and just listen to your thoughts? Do you go crazy like I feel I'm doing right now?"

"Why do you feel like you're going crazy?"

"My thoughts are driving me crazy! Why can't I think like a normal person? Why can't my brain stay on one thought? Why can't it be a happy thought? Depressive thought after depressive thought. What is wrong with me?" I got up and walked out. First session complete.

I got into my car and turned it on. *Marcus, just breathe.* Ok, I thought I was ready to talk to someone. I'm obviously wrong. I now feel embarrassed for giving that an attempt. I'm supposed to be able to figure things out. The vulnerability scares me. I felt emotionally wide open to get punched.

What do I think love is? Great, now that question is going to be on my mind all day. It makes me upset that I don't have a definition for it. He wasn't supposed to ask me that. He's supposed to be helping me, not making me more confused. How am I supposed to open up about Camille if we never get to that point in the conversation? I probably should turn around, drive back there and finish our session. Walking out was my initial reaction, which exposes my tendency to stay guarded.

"What's your definition of love?" I asked. Camille is looking at her finger nails, which signals that she's nervous, at least in my opinion. I now feel I must ask everyone that question. The psychiatrist now has the question stuck in my head. Is he my psychiatrist or my therapist? Calling him a therapist sounds better. I can't believe I actually went to see one. I don't understand the stigma behind it now that I've went. My first session didn't go well, but I can see the benefits of it.

"My definition of love. What an interesting question."

"Well, are you going to answer it?" I asked. Her energy is telling me she doesn't want to answer the question. Why is this a question she wants to avoid? Maybe she's like me. Maybe she doesn't have an answer. Maybe it's something that can't be explained and I'm not crazy.

"Love is caring for someone more than you care about yourself. No, I take that back, that's too strong. I'll use you and me as an example. If I love you, I'm going to consciously give you all of me and trust you not to abuse my love. It's our world, and every moment counts even when we're not together physically. My responsibility is to be there for you in every way possible. I'm supposed to make you happy."

"So...." she put her hand up, cutting me off.

"If every moment counts, and I'm supposed to make you happy, I have to keep you on my mind and stay aware of my actions that could affect our moments together. I'm probably naïve, but I feel like love can be perfect on my part. I don't believe in making mistakes when I truly care for a person. How can I go do something that's going to affect the moments we spend together, even if I don't get caught? Internally, I'm not going to be happy. What type of person would that make me?"

"I don't know what to say."

"I feel we give ourselves space to make mistakes because internally we truly know if we're ready to be with a person or not, we just don't like to be alone. Let's say you get into a relationship, fall for a person, but then become interested in another person. The simple solution would be for the person to leave their significant other, correct?"

"I'm listening."

"The first excuse is you don't want to hurt the person, but aren't you hurting the person either way? Is it really you don't love the person, you're just comfortable with the person and want to have them for insurance?"

"Some people love differently," I replied.

"So, you believe you can be in love with a significant other and constantly cheat on the person?"

"You do know I have a significant other, correct?" I asked with a smile.

"But you don't love her anymore. You just don't know how to leave her, not to be with me, but to just be happy." Her statement has me stuck, not knowing what to say. I believe I still love Tiffany. Let me rephrase that, I do love Tiffany. I'm not cheating on her, it's more like I'm cheating on life right now, and she just happens to be a part of it. I'm not sure how to respond to her definition of love.

"How do you think I feel about Tiffany?" I asked. I'm not sure if it's proper to talk about my significant other with the girl I currently have feelings for, but here I am. How did I get to this point of confusion in life?

"That's a great question. Well, I'm not actually there, so it's hard to give a definitive answer. From the outside looking in it seems like you care about her, but have been opened to what the world has to offer, and it has you curious. Curiosity can be a gift and a curse, depending on your perspective on life. Chasing curiosity usually requires change of your surroundings, and people tend to not like change. People have a bad habit of wanting their cake and ice cream too."

"So, I should leave Tiffany to chase the curiosity?"

"Am I the curiosity?" she asked seductively. I feel myself becoming erect. Is she flirting or being serious? Either way, I like what she's doing. My phone is ringing. Whoa, it's Misha. Why is she calling me? She never calls me, though I consider her my favorite cousin. I'm not answering the call. If it's important she will send me a text message. How awkward would it be to answer the phone telling Misha I'm hanging out with Camille? I didn't tell her Camille and I were talking. The call threw off my train of thought. What was I just thinking about?

"I totally forgot what we were talking about," I truthfully admitted. "The phone call threw me off. It was a family member who usually doesn't call."

"On a scale of one to ten, what would you rate your caring for Tiffany?" I took a deep breath. Am I supposed to truthfully answer this question? My life is slowly but surely turning into a lie and I want to reverse that. I feel myself losing my grip on life and want to gain back control. How do I gain back control? I have no clue. At least I'm aware that I'm losing control over it, if that even matters.

"I would say a nine," I truthfully replied. Her eyes widened. "I care about Tiffany on a deep level."

"I could have sworn you told me you were thinking about leaving her when we were at the restaurant." I can't distinguish Camille's tone.

"Because I wanted to leave her means I can't deeply care about her?" I feel this conversation going in the wrong direction. Maybe I should have given a different answer. I should have said five.

"Why would you leave if you deeply care?" The question stings. I'm leaving because I have feelings for her. Isn't that obvious? Or is she playing mind games? "And are we going to avoid the obvious conversation?"

"What's the obvious conversation?" She squinted her eyes at me. What conversation is she talking about? Am I missing something?

"You know what conversation I'm referring to."

"Please, enlighten me."

"My change, my secret." I now feel stuck. Why must she bring this up? I was trying not to think about it, hoping it would go away. I guess I'm taking habits from my mom. I concluded that my initial reaction was wrong. I don't know how to process the information. I don't want to start letting it sink into my mind. Now I need a drink. This is when I start thinking too much with a bunch of unsorted thoughts. I feel a headache coming.

"There's nothing to discuss," I stated. I wish I had a topic so I can quickly change the subject, but I don't. I'm now stuck in this awkward position. Seriously, what are we supposed to discuss?

"There's nothing to discuss?" Camille asked. "Are you serious? There's everything to discuss. You must have unanswered questions. You have to, it's impossible not to. So, now is the time to ask them."

"I have no questions." She stood up. If this is her way of saying she's going to leave, then she's in for a rude awakening if she thinks I'm going to stop her. This is a new experience and new situation. This situation has never been in one of my dreams, not even a daydream. Just thinking……. I'm not going to think on it. I know myself well. Why even put myself in a situation where I could mentally go insane. I'm not putting myself through that, and if that makes me selfish then oh well. I've been called worse words.

"Marcus, we can't run away from this." She sat back down. "We have to talk about it." I stood up. If I wanted counseling I'd go call my therapist. Why can't we go with the flow? Is that too much to ask for? There's no underlying issue. We're both just living right now. "Marcus, may you please sit back down and talk to me? I want to work things out with you."

"What is there to work out?" I have no plans of sitting back down. "I'm fine, you're fine, everything's fine." She stood up. I now want to sit down, but will not be petty. "I don't understand how we arrived to this point. How about we go catch a movie. Better yet, we can go to a football game. My old high school has a big game today. I'd love to see them."

"Fine, if you don't want to talk about it, then we won't. We will act like it doesn't exist. How about we act like I never told you, like that day never happened. You'll never be able to say I didn't try to talk about it. Please don't try to bring it up in the future."

"I won't," I bluntly stated. She shook her head and walked away.

****

"How do you feel about transgenders?" I asked my co-worker. We've been working beside each other for years. This may be the first time I've asked him a thoughtful question. We usually talk about insignificant things like sports.

"Whoa," he started, "That's a random, deep question." He took a deep breath. "I'll put it this way, I think anyone who blatantly tells the world that they're not happy with how God, the universe, or whatever they may believe in, has created them…. You should definitely be aware of the type of person you're dealing with on a mental level. This just may be a personal answer on my behalf. I like to pay attention to how people think, which means I pay attention to actions because most actions come from a thought. And if it's a long, thorough thought, that means you're telling yourself a certain story."

"Wow."

"Sorry if I got deep. I'm not even sure if I answered your question. That's my answer without actually answering, if that makes sense. What made you ask me such a random question?"

"My girlfriend watches crazy shows. She had me watching a weird show last night that had a character that was acting as a transgender. Interesting show to say the least."

"I really think that community is growing quickly. I'm referring to the transgenders. Luckily, I'm already married so it's something I'm not really bothered by. A person can do whatever makes them happy at the end of the day. If I had to give a firm answer I'd say there's nothing wrong with it. Putting all my beliefs aside, who's to say God don't make mistakes? I can look at things from both sides. How do you feel towards transgenders?"

"Would you feel the same way if you were single?" I asked, purposely ignoring his question. Great, his phone just rang. Today has been slow, now all of a sudden it wants to start getting busy when I'm seeking advice and insight. I'm in a weird spot emotionally, a horrible place mentally, and a crushed place spiritually. I need to start soul searching. Too bad that the only way I know how to soul search is through the bottle. I need to call my mom. We need to set up a drinking session. How I'm currently feeling, I'll probably break down and cry while drinking. I don't remember the last time I cried while being an adult.

I used to drink while on my lunch break. It was during a period when I guess I was self-sabotaging. I was constantly thinking about the past, knowing it would make me unhappy. It seemed like a cycle of thoughts I couldn't let go of, or maybe I didn't want to let go. Maybe it was just my excuse to have a reason to drink while on my break. One day I decided to stop doing it, but the sabotage hasn't stopped. I don't know how to deal with it so I now just try to mask the emotions. Smiling usually covers the anger or sadness I'm experiencing. How can I be honest with anyone when I can barely be honest with myself?

I just received a text message from Tiffany saying she loves me. Though my life has been a lie to an extent, lying directly to her actually hurts my heart. For example, I've never denied me being an alcoholic to her, I've just never mentioned it. I've told a lot of those types of lies. Are those considered lies? These direct lies are new and I sleep with a guilty conscience. The simple solution would be to stop the lies. Unfortunately, life isn't simple. Let me get back into work.

"Baby, did you receive my text message?" I'm at Tiffany's place and she's making dinner tonight. Here goes another situation when the lie sounds so much better than the truth. The truth would be that yes, I did receive the text message, but didn't text back because I wasn't sure if I loved her at that moment. But that would be harsh, right? If I love her, how can I currently be cheating on her? I really feel I'm the only person with this thought process and people will never understand why I sometimes feel like I'm losing my mind.

"I did not, but will admit I need a new phone and have been moving slow towards getting one. This phone I have now has been acting weird. It works when it wants to. What did the text message say?"

"I was telling you that I love you." She smiled and went back to cooking. I want to admit to Tiffany what I did. A part of me wants to tell her I made a mistake, the other part of me wants to tell her it's over between the two of us. I really need someone to vent to. I'm scared of my thoughts sometimes, so I really need for someone to be able to read my thoughts while they're still in my brain, and just solve them for me. Is that too much to ask for?

"I love you too." Thank God she's not looking back at me. She would see the confusion on my face as I sit at the dining room table. How do you fall out of love with a person who has done nothing wrong? Not only have I fallen out of love with a special person, I've fallen out of love with Tiffany for a…..I need a drink. No, I need a whole bottle. I want to wash the thoughts away, even if it's temporarily.

Tiffany placed my plate of meat loaf, rice, and green beans on the table and sat across from me. I've lost my appetite. The reality is starting to sink in and I'm trying hard to fight the thought. Maybe Camille is playing a sick joke on me. Maybe she's trying to see under what measures would I leave her. Maybe she's testing my loyalty. If I stick around, she will reward me in the end for knowing that nothing can break us apart. Yes, that's what's going on.

"I had the oddest idea about two days ago," Tiffany started. "I actually wanted to get your name tattooed on me." I looked up from eating. "Yes, I know it's a crazy thought considering I've said a million times that I'll never get a tattoo. That day I thought it would be the truest form of loyalty."

"I'm happy you didn't do that. That would have been a very bad idea." A look of displeasure is on her face. I hope that face doesn't mean that she's already accomplished getting the tattoo.

"Why would that have been a bad idea? I feel like it's the closest bond of loyalty next to marriage. Getting someone's name put on you really means you have no plans of ever leaving them."

"Plans do have a way of changing." I took a bite from the meat loaf. Tiffany has anger on her face and she isn't trying to hide it. I probably should have worded my answer differently.

"What in the hell is that supposed to mean?" she angrily asked.

"What? Plans don't change in people's lives? It does happen sometimes. Feelings sometimes change. Sometimes people grow apart. A person may connect with an outside individual and feel like that's the person they really want to be with. Then that puts the person in a tough spot because of their heightened level of loyalty. Him or her could feel loyal to the tattoo, which then makes them loyal to the person who they now realize isn't the right one."

"Marcus, I'm talking about us!"

"Now you're in a loop of unhappiness because you see the tattoo every day. The reality is you should probably leave, but since you've gotten the tattoo you've painted a different story of the person inside of your head. The person may actually be a good person, but the new individual you've met is the right one. Your mind won't allow you to accept that fact because you now have a permanent mark of someone's name. The name will be there forever, and that could ultimately lead to a series of more regrets."

"Marcus! What in the hell are you talking about?" I blinked three times. "You looked like you were possessed while talking. I'm referring to us. We are made for each other. Neither of us are going anywhere. Plans do tend to change, except when it God's plan. We are God's plan. Some things are meant to be. We are, and don't you ever think differently."

"I know we are meant for each other." I touched her hand. "I think if we weren't made for each other we would have ended a long time ago. These have been some of the best years of my life. Everything hasn't been perfect, but I believe real situations aren't perfect."

"Wow, we've really been together for a few years. Time goes by fast when you're having a good time. I pray we have a lot more years together."

"We will." I picked up her hand and kissed it. "We will."

****

"Promise me you'll never leave." I nodded my head. The warmth of her being on top of me. I'm in a trance, a trance I don't want to escape. The moments are strong. I don't know what force is behind it, but I wish it would let me go. I don't want it to let me go but this type of pull is dangerous. How is it possible to feel this way? "Marcus, stay in the moment. Don't think your way out of it. Do you want to go again?" I nodded my head. The high sex drive, how can I get enough? Any emptiness I experience, she temporarily fills. Why can't it be permanently? I should leave Tiffany, sooner than later.

My phone is ringing, it's my mom. I quickly pushed Camille off me. No one comes before mom. "Yes Mom," I happily answered.

"Son, is it weird that I don't want anything, don't want a conversation, I just wanted to hear your voice?" I have to use that line on Tiffany. That line will always work. Mom's voice just snapped me back into reality. I'm with a woman who my mom has no clue about. Another reminder I'm living a lie. Why must my thought process be this way?

"No mom, it's not weird. I'm happy to hear your voice also. Is everything Ok? We need to get together and maybe go to a restaurant, or maybe hang out at your house?"

"That will be fine. I just wanted to hear your voice. I'll let you continue your day. I love you." The call ended. Maybe that was my cue to get out of here. I look at everything as a sign for the most part. Do I listen to the sign every time? Of course not.

"You must really love your mom," Camille said as she cuddled next to me.

"More than anyone or anything else in the world. I may love her more than myself. I pray I die before her. There's no way I'd survive if the opposite happened. I would go crazy, literally. I'm not in denial about it either. Someone would have to put me in the place where they put the crazy people. I couldn't imagine not being with her. She's like my living angel. Talking to her always puts things in perspective for me. She reminds me that things are only as big as I make them."

"I heard that men that have good relationships with their moms are great people to settle down with," Camille said with a smile. I nodded my head in agreement. I'm not sure if Camille is aware of it, but she really says the weirdest things at the wrong times. I guess I'm the only one that's aware of the fact that I have a great relationship with my mom, but am cheating on my significant other. My mood just switched from happy to sad.

Chapter 3

Dear Diary,

I love him, if that's even possible. I told myself I'd never let me fall for another woman's man. Matter of fact, I PROMISED myself I'd never let me fall for another woman's man. How did I allow this to happen? How did I give all my power over to him? When I was a man I judged those types of women. I called them stupid bitches. Now look, I'm exactly one of them. Damn. I think it's because he accepts me, though he hasn't told me or even admitted it to himself yet. I can feel it in my soul. He truly loves me. He truly cares for me. I've never felt this type of feeling before. It has to be real. Now it leaves me in a strange position. I would never ruin his relationship, I'm not that type of woman. What if he never leaves her? What if he never talks to me again? What if he lies to himself for the rest of his life and marries her? What will that do to him mentally? Yes, I care about his thoughts and wellbeing. He said she hasn't done anything to make him leave her, but what about me? What did I do to deserve this? Did I ask for it? Should I've not decided to be his friend, though I found him attractive? I had no intention of things going further. Now I'm stuck, fighting for the best, but preparing for the worst. My gut says he'll never leave. I'm not trusting my gut. My gut is negative. I'm trying to have faith. I'm trying to be positive. I'm so confused right now; my emotions are everywhere. Happiness, that's all I want. Is that too much to ask for? God, just give him to me. I promise to treat him right, treat him like a king. He's the missing piece to complete my puzzle. How are you going to place the missing piece into my life, then not let me have it? Does that make you or me the selfish one?

Camille

I closed the tablet. Did she leave this out purposely? Maybe I'm just being nosy. She loves me, great. She's sure I love her, though I've never told her. Now I'm forced to ask myself do I love her too. It's too soon to be using that word. Do I have feelings for her? Of course I do. Am I able to describe my feelings towards her? I can't, or maybe I just don't want to. Did I really tell her that Tiffany hasn't done anything to make me leave her? I thought I only keep that thought in my brain. I'm becoming vulnerable. Everything about life is confusing. I find myself wanting to sit in a corner and cry for hours, but my pride won't let me. The answers won't come to me from crying. I have to figure things out.

"What would you like to do today?" Camille asked as she walked into the living room. I shrugged my shoulders. My mind is elsewhere. I really want to sit somewhere and have a couple of drinks. She really loves me. "Don't shrug your shoulders at me. I need answers. What's on your mind. You don't seem like you want to be here today? Did I do something wrong?"

"I read your tablet." Her eyes widened.

"Is that right?"

"I probably shouldn't have opened it, but curiosity was killing me. I was interested in what type of writing you were doing." She picked up the tablet.

"Well, did you read the next page?" She handed me the tablet.

"No, I didn't. The first page put me into enough deep thought. I also felt guilty for reading it." I opened the tablet and looked at the next page.

Dear Diary,

I'm sad and realizing that I may be living in a fantasy world. My last entry to you may have been a lot of imagining and wishful thinking. The thought has been lingering in my mind and I'm trying to fight off the thought. I have this way with reality that when I don't agree with it, I try to dismiss it by convincing myself that reality is wrong. What if he truly never accepts me? Was I better off not telling him? Since graduating high school my life has been a secret. I've always wanted to bond with a person, share my inner thoughts and just be accepted. Was I better off just having sex with him? I've had sex with other men, but to spiritually connect with a person, it's a feeling that I can't describe, but do know that's what I'm experiencing with Marcus.

With that being said, I'm still scared to let him have ALL of me. He's become my drug. With drugs, you become dependent. So, if I'm counting on him to give me highs, it's only right that he's going to give me lows also. I'm all alone in this world. I ask myself if it's by choice or force. Maybe it's both? Sometimes I ask myself has my secret caused me to live a lie? Or has my secret caused me to be able to create a new truth? I experience my real feelings when Marcus is around. I hang around other men and women, but they don't give me that feeling of completeness. To go from feeling complete to feeling unaccepted is a crushing blow to the heart. I shouldn't have told him. He's the only man I've told. Why would I do such a thing?

Camille

"So, what do you think?" Camille asked. I closed the tablet and took a deep breath.

"Honestly, I don't know what to think anymore. Life has become a spiral of confusion for me. This is coming from someone who prides himself on being able to figure life out. I'm supposed to have most of the answers."

"Do you think I can be a girl that completes you as much as you complete me?" I took another deep breath.

"I honestly don't know what to believe." I got up and walked towards the front door. "Maybe I'll come back, maybe I won't." I opened the door and walked out.

****

"How are you, Mom?" I passed the bottle of Hennessy. We have beer, vodka, tequila, and everything else. No cups, all cans and bottles. We'll more than likely go through all of it. Nothing will be left over. The past week has been a blur. I haven't been drinking but have been going through the motions. I know I've avoided all contact with Camille. I've saw Tiffany but can't recall the moments together. I've been a conscious zombie.

"Would you believe me if I told you I still cry myself to sleep every night?" She passed the bottle back to me after taking a few swallows.

"No, I would not believe that. We never talk about it, but I can still feel the sad energy you give off. I figured it may be because you don't talk about it."

"Well son, I do. I cry myself to sleep every night. Even when I'm with another man, I still cry myself to sleep. Which is why I haven't had any lasting relationships. It's not fair to the man. How do you accept your husband, the father of your child, cheating on you with another man? How do you even process that in a positive way? Marcus, I never cheated on him, never lied to him, I was his servant. It's very similar to how Tiffany treats you." I just caught the chills. "Are the good ones supposed to suffer while the bad ones prosper?"

"It definitely seems that way, mom." The tears are starting to form in her eyes. My face may not be showing it, but I really want to cry right now. It's all making sense now. It's really sinking in that I'm just like my dad. How is that even possible? How can I emulate the man I hate so much, all the way down to cheating on my queen with a….. I feel my heart beating fast.

Camille has been texting nonstop since I left her apartment. I haven't texted her back, but I also haven't deleted or blocked her number. What am I telling myself? Why haven't the feelings erased? Why hasn't the hate for Camille grown stronger? Why isn't there any hate at all? Am I skipping over the reality of the matter? I'm still hoping for the joke.

"Marcus, what are you thinking about? You look like you're in deep thought over there. You've even stopped drinking the liquor. At least pass the bottle back." I passed the bottle. I hate when I get so deep into thought that I forget the moment I'm in.

"Mom, I think I'm going to propose to Tiffany. I take that back, I'm definitely going to propose to Tiffany. You're the first and only person to know. Keep it that way." Mom smiled, nodded her head, and took a few swallows of the liquor. What in the hell did I just do?

****

"Will you marry me?" I'm really down on one knee, ring in my hand, in front of Tiffany and all of her co-workers at her job. Tears are in her eyes. I wish I could read her thoughts. Actually, I wish she could read my thoughts.

"Yes, I will," she happily replied. I stood up and kissed her. If she could read my thoughts, she would definitely give me a different answer. My phone is ringing. Great, it's Camille. She's interfering with the flow of positive energy that's in the air right now. Well, at least that's the type of energy I'm trying to give off. Why won't she see the sign I'm trying to give? I'm currently just living life, not putting much thought into anything. My reasoning to myself is that life has a way of figuring itself out. I just proposed to a woman I was seriously contemplating leaving a few weeks ago. I've been experiencing more headaches, which is very unusual. I need help.

"I'm so happy for the two of you," Tiffany's female coworker happily said. "You two make a great couple. I know you will have a long-lasting marriage." I forced a smile and nodded my head. I'm happy she's so confident, because I'm not.

"Marcus, how do you feel about me?" Camille asked.

"I'm not sure," I coldly replied.

"How can you not be sure about YOUR feelings?"

"I'm getting married." She gasped. "I proposed to Tiffany."

"Why would you do that? You've read my diary. You know my thoughts. You know how I feel."

"Because I love her."

"You love me!" I just caught the chills. "Marcus, you don't love her."

"How are you going to tell me how I feel about her? She's done nothing but treat me right, love me, and…… been everything I could have ever wanted. You already know this."

"But here you are, sitting in a car with me." Her hand touched my thigh. I'm instantly erect. She unbuttoned my pants. "Are you sure you love her?" She put her mouth onto my dick.

"Get out," I coldly stated. She lifted up her head.

"Marcus....."

"Please, get out." She shook her head, opened the door and slammed it as she exited. I think I just want to sit here and cry for a while. I've been wanting to cry more often, and if I add that with all the headaches I'm experiencing, what does that say about the direction of my life? I tell myself I can gain control of everything, but that may be just to make me feel good about myself. Sometimes lying to yourself keeps your spirit alive.

I hate when my phone ringing wakes me up out of a good sleep. Nothing irks my soul more. Who could be calling me this early? It can't be Tiffany. I usually send her a good morning text when we don't wake up with each other. It's my cousin, Janae. She never calls me. What in the hell does she want this early in the morning. "Hello," I annoyingly answered.

"Marcus, your mom is in the hospital." I'm stuck, literally. *Marcus, don't react, just breathe.* "She's in a coma." *Marcus, don't react, just breathe.* "I'm going to text you the address to the hospital she's at." My thoughts are numb, if that's even possible. I don't want to process the information I just received. I'm going to go back to sleep and start over. This must be a horrible dream. "Marcus, are you there?" *Breathe Marcus, please just breathe.* "Hello? Marcus?" I ended the call. I still don't know what to think, and since that's the case, I'm just going to lay here and look at the ceiling.

I walked into the hospital and walked towards the room number I received in the text message. My body is numb. I'm following my advice and just breathing. There is no fear, no anxiety, no emotion, just numbness. I've never been to the hospital before, and can only go by how they portray these types of scenes on TV. I've never felt this way about a situation so serious.

I walked into Mom's hospital room. She looks like she's just sleeping peacefully. There's still a numbness over me. I won't allow myself to feel anything. My mom is really in a coma. No, she's just taking a nap. I moved a chair by her bed and sat down.

What brought her to this point? I want to ask the doctor, but don't want to hear the answer. She looks the same. It doesn't look like anything is wrong with her. I feel the sadness coming. The thought cycle of blaming myself is about to happen. I can feel it. I guess this would be a good time to talk to her. Let me text Tiffany and tell her my mom is in the hospital.

"Oh no, this can't be." I turned around. Wow, I'm speechless. I can't believe what I'm seeing right now. You'd think after eighteen years I'd be looking forward to this moment. Now that it's occurring, I wish it wouldn't have happened. It's my dad. My fucking dad is really here. "Hi son," he said as he walked towards the bed. He stopped and touched Mom's hand.

"Hi," I said back. I can't recall of many times I've been at a loss for words. This time is one of them. My dad is really here in the flesh. He still looks the same, just slightly older. I now feel shy like I'm a kid again. I've planned different scenarios on what would happen if I ever saw him again. It's going nothing like how I visualized it in my head.

"What happened?" he asked.

"I'm not sure. I just got here. I received the news she's here from my cousin. That was around an hour ago. I haven't really given myself a chance to process everything yet."

"How are you doing?"

"I'm fine," I quickly replied. There's now silence. He's probably thinking of what to say next. He may even be wondering if he should say anything at all, which isn't a bad thought. Don't say anything, just stand there in silence. We both can be in the same room and not say anything. That would be fine to me. There's so many words that need to be said that it may actually be better not to say anything at all.

"It's been a while," he started, breaking the silence, "Maybe we should grab some coffee one day this week and catch up. There's a lot of catching up we need to do. We may be having coffee for hours." He smiled and put his hand on my shoulder. His hand being on my shoulder brings me back to the happy days when I was a kid, the memories before the liquor came in. I only remember a few, but they are there.

"We can do that," I said with a smile.

"I know this won't be an easy process, and it shouldn't be, but I want to be back in your life. If you deny me, that's totally understandable. You probably should deny me, but seeing your mom like this has put everything in perspective. What I did was really fucked up."

"Is she okay?" I turned around. It's a brown skinned man with a younger boy of the same complexion. Who are these two people? My dad's demeanor has totally changed. His expression now displays anger. The two approached us.

"I specifically told you not to come up here," Dad angrily said. What is going on right now?

"I'm sorry," the man said back. "I was worried. I wanted to know what was going on. Please, lower your tone with me." Dad turned towards me.

"Son, this is my husband." I feel the same numbness I felt while coming here. 'Wow' is all I really want to say. "And this is our adopted son, Brandon." I'm beyond speechless. I got up and walked out. I need to get myself together. Today has to be one long nightmare. I should have gone back to sleep this morning like I planned on doing. This day can't get any worse. I'm going to go home and try not to cry. I will not cry. *Marcus, be an adult and walk back in there.* I want to listen to that voice in my head, but the greater voice says to ignore it. There's so many thoughts running through my head at the moment. I will ignore each thought. I'm tired of thinking for the day.

"Marcus, I have emotions too, you know? You can't decide to leave for good then suddenly show back up without weeks of communication." I walked past her and sat on the couch.

"Camille, please just let me sit down and get my thoughts together. Being alone probably isn't a wise decision on my part right now, so I came here."

"What about your fiancé?" she asked with an attitude. "That's who you should be running to. I mean, she is your better half. You are going to MARRY her." She's probably right. I've just realized that every time I go through a problem Camille is my first choice to run to. I said I was tired of thinking for today, and what do I do? I go to a place to do exactly what I'm tired of doing.

"Camille, may you please shut up for five minutes! I'll argue with you once I get my thoughts together."

"You're at my place! I don't have to shut up!" I stood up.

"You're right, you don't have to shut up. My dad popped back up today. I just needed somewhere to run away to for a few hours. I'll find another place." I walked out. I guess I'll go sit down at a park.

The park is a peaceful place, especially when all the kids are at school. It's a place where I can just sit down and enjoy the little things about life. There's the trees, the clouds in the sky, the things we tend to overlook on a daily basis. Sometimes it's good to just sit and take it all in. It tends to remind me that when everything seems wrong there's always something to be happy for. At least I'm breathing.

"Marcus?" I looked up. "Holy shit, it's really you!"

"Christina?" I stood up. "Is that really you?" We hugged each other. She smells good. "What are you doing here? I'm referring to this park. I come to this park from time to time. I've never seen you here." Her pale skin has a different type of glow. She looks slightly different from the last time I saw her, though it was years ago. I remember her having blonde hair, it's now burgundy.

"I come here sometimes too, and I've never seen you here. We must have bad timing on catching each other here. I stay nearby. Let's go to my place and catch up. I'm sure we have a lot to talk about. This may sound crazy but I still call you my best friend. People always think something is wrong with me since they don't know you. To them you seem like a ghost. You ride with me, I'll bring you back to your car. This way saves gas." I nodded my head and followed her to her car.

We walked into her house. Her house is squeaky clean like she has a maid that comes to clean it daily, at least downstairs.

I'm not sure what upstairs looks like. "It's not hard to keep a clean home when you live alone," she said as if she can read my mind. "Make yourself at home. I have to go upstairs and grab my phone charger." I sat down on the living room couch. Christina has left her notebook open. I'm sure she won't mind if I read it.

Dear Diary,

Sex deprived, not sure if it's more by choice, or by force. I'm not in denial about the fact that something is wrong with me. I'm a recovering addict from everything. When I say everything, I mean EVERYTHING. Weed, liquor, cocaine, pills. You name it, I've tried it. Those last four were severe addictions though. Seven years of daily heavy use, I wonder why I'm alive. I'm only twenty-three and feel like I'm fucked for life. For seven years, any sex I had, I had while under the influence of something. Now that I'm off (trying to stay off) it's like I don't get horny. It's like I can't get horny. My hormones are at an all-time low. What is wrong with me? Will I be this way forever? Being sober sucks if that's the case. I'm trying to be normal. I've been asking myself what in the hell does "normal" consist of? Thinking with a clear mind is scary. Reality is fucking scary. My psychiatrist has me on all these pills that's supposed to be helping me. All those drugs I was on made me develop symptoms of being bi-polar, schizophrenia, having ADHD, depression, and a whole bunch of other shit I wish I didn't have to know about having. The main one I hate is being clinically depressed. You hear a lot of people saying they're depressed, but they're really just sad. I have nine different prescriptions. The inner me says that I've been an addict to illegal drugs, just to become an addict to legal drugs. I then tell myself that the inner me is fucked up and to never listen to that voice. All I hear is voices in my head to be honest. It's hard to distinguish which is a good or bad voice. Depression talks to me the most. I know his voice clearly. He talks to me a lot. It's to the point that I consider the voice a friend. When he gets quiet for too long I ask where's he at. The voice makes me comfortable while being sober, maybe because it feels real. Hold on, did I basically answer my first sentence of this entry?

Christina

"You're the only person I've let read that, though I didn't tell you to read it." I put the tablet down.

"Christina, what went wrong? Why do I feel like I've let you down?"

"Because you're a narcissist and make everyone's problem somehow, someway, revolve around you." I shook my head. She may have a point. I haven't seen her in six years, and it seems like that's when things started going wrong. We were best friends since elementary school up until that point.

"Excuse me for having a heart," I said.

"You should stop having a heart. Having a heart gets you hurt."

"I don't think you understand how true your last statement was. It made my heart sting."

"I went seven years without feelings, going through numbness. My memory is really damaged. My friends would tell me what happened the night before, I would have no recollection of it. I try not to believe what they told me, but they put images in my head. If it's true that my "friends" would let me do those types of things..... well fuck them too."

"Were the things you did considered bad?" I asked.

"I'd rather not talk about it. I just tell myself that it's all a lie since I don't remember feeling any of it. I can't put myself at the scene of any of those situations, but then my best friend comes and tells me that it's all true. I have anti-depressant pills but don't want to take them. Marcus, am I crazy?"

"I'm the wrong person to ask."

"What? The narcissist doesn't have an answer? You always have an answer, even if it's the wrong one."

"I'm not a narcissist," I bluntly said. Though I've called myself one, I don't want anyone else calling me that. It's funny, Christina may know me better than any other person besides my mom. She knows about my drinking problem.

"Are you still an alcoholic?" she asked. She's reading my mind.

"I am," I happily replied.

"How does your girlfriend accept that? I'm assuming you have one."

"She doesn't, only because she doesn't know."

"How in the heck doesn't she know? You basically have alcoholic written across your forehead." She laughed and shook her head.

"I guess that only applies to other alcoholics. Tiffany has never been drunk before. She's never tried any drugs. My baby is pure."

"Why are you cheating on her?" Fear just shot into my heart. My face isn't showing it.

"What makes you say that?" I asked with surprise in my voice.

"Marcus, I've known you since I was five. I don't care how damaged I've become as a person on the inside, it hasn't stopped me from still knowing everything about you. The drugs haven't affected that part of me to be connected to you." I now hate that I've known her for so long. It's true, we are connected, and it's an unbreakable connection. Not a connection based off sex, we've never had that before. Just a connection off bonding and always being there for each other ever since we were kids. She's been out of my life for six years, but I'm happy she's back. I'd known she started smoking weed, but didn't know she was experimenting with other drugs.

"Christina, where have you been for the past six years?" I asked. Yes, I'm trying to change the subject. One thing I've learned is that people love talking about themselves and their situation. Sometimes you just have to switch the focus back to the person. "The last time I spoke to you, you were visiting a relative in Michigan."

"Marcus, you're trying to change the subject!" I now see that none of my words will work with her. I now also see that none of my ways will work on her. I thought I'd created good tactics while she was away. I guess they're not good enough. "Who is the other woman?"

"There is no other woman," I calmly replied.

"So, you're going to stand there and lie to me?"

"Christina, you haven't even met my girlfriend. You didn't even know I had a girlfriend. How are you going to accuse me of having another woman when you don't know who my original woman is?" I laughed. "Women and their intuition."

"Marcus, do you remember when we were six and promised we'd never lie to each other? Well, you're breaking that promise." I've just realized that I've never lied to her until today. Wow, maybe we are meant to be friends.

"So, you're not going to tell me where you've been for the past six years? You left me hanging when I needed you the most."

"Marcus! You can't answer my question with a question!" She closed her eyes, then opened them. "Yes, Bryan, I know."

"Who is Bryan?" I asked. She's talking, but her eyes aren't in my direction.

"Bryan! I know! It's going to be fine."

"CHRISTINA!" I hollered. She slightly jumped.

"Shit, I'm sorry. I was talking to Bryan. That's the name I gave to the voice of depression." I now feel sad. You can see it in my eyes. I don't know why I feel sad, I just do. I feel guilty. "That's where I've been, somewhere losing my mind. Somewhere having full conversations with voices."

"At least you're not in a psych ward."

"I've definitely been there too during these past six years." My mouth just dropped open. "Marcus, if you only knew half of what I've been through these past couple of years. You may be the same Marcus from our childhood, but I'm not the same Christina. It sometimes makes me cry when I realize how damaged I am as a person. Bryan tells me I'm damaged beyond repair. I believe him on most days. How can you not respect a person's honesty?"

"I..... I don't know what to say."

"You know shit is real when the narcissist doesn't know what to say."

"You're going to stop calling me a narcissist," I laughed. Part of me wants to tell Christina everything. I know I can trust her with my secrets. The reality is that I hate telling myself the truth because sometimes the truth doesn't make sense.

"I'm so glad I ran into you. I feel like I've found a part of me that's been missing. We have so much history. Marcus, you've always had the ability to make me happy. I'm not sure if you still have that ability now that we're adults. We're going to figure things out and get back on the same page. I know there's a reason we've connected again."

"We will get back on the same page," I said. "We have to learn each other again, and to distract me from the ugliness in my life, I'll say I'm up for the challenge. So, where do we start?"

"Do you remember when I was such a balanced person?" I nodded my head. "Things have changed, I'm now either extremely to the left or right. I'm either sleeping for twelve hours or staying up for two days with no sleep. I either really love a guy, or I extremely hate him. I'm either heavily starving myself or I'm eating like I'm 400 pounds, though I only weigh 160."

"Well, it seems like we have a lot of catching up to do." She nodded her head. This should be fun.

****

"What made you propose?" Tiffany asked.

"Huh?" I hate when I answer immediately without putting in any thought. The question has caught me by surprise. Who asks these types of questions? Is this really what women think about?

"What made you propose?" she asked again.

"What type of question is that?"

"A question that I would like a response to? I know this may be bad timing because your mom is in the hospital. The question has been on my mind heavily."

"How am I supposed to answer that?"

"So, you just woke up and decided you wanted to marry me?" Today has been an interesting day to say the least. We're at the same restaurant where Camille broke the news to me, only in a different corner. The mind-blowing part is that we've never been to this restaurant before. We've passed by it plenty of times, but today Tiffany decided she wanted to try it out. To say that I'm scared would actually be a lie. I'm more than scared, I'm terrified. I may not display this on the outside, but on the inside, I'm shaking.

"Pretty much," I sarcastically replied. She rolled her eyes. "Why does that matter?" I really want to avoid this conversation. I should change the subject next time it's my turn to speak. My mom is in the hospital, why does she want to ask these types of questions? I haven't mentioned my dad to her. Too much is going on at once.

"It was definitely a surprise. We've never talked about marriage before, though we've been together for a while. I'm not saying I'm changing my mind, because I'll never forget the moment, but now that my excitement has gone down and it's starting to sink in, I just find it odd." I was hoping the excitement would last longer. Tiffany is doing the one thing I fell in love with her over. She's a deep thinker. She's a logical thinker, not thinking with only her emotions. What I love her for is coming back to bite me.

"Just because we've never discussed it doesn't mean I don't love you and want to be with you forever." I leaned over and kissed her. My mind is in a weird place, or maybe I'm just having a conscience. Kissing her now feels wrong. I've had my lips on another person's lips, another person's body, and now have brought Camille's lips back to her. I've never cheated, so maybe it's normal to have these thoughts. But these thoughts were nonexistent until Camille revealed her supposed secret. The secret is not real so the guilt should be nonexistent. Is it possible I'm going crazy? My thoughts seem to be spiraling out of control, or maybe I'm just thinking too much.

"I love you too," she happily said, "And always will." I'm scanning the restaurant wishing I had the ability to remember faces. I feel like all eyes are on me, considering I passed out the last time I was here. "Have you thought about the wedding? Any ideas? Do you have a date in mind? Do you have an idea for the honeymoon? Not saying that we have to go with all of your ideas."

"Of course I have ideas." That's a lie on my part. I honestly haven't thought of any of it. "I saw my dad at the hospital." Tiffany's eyes widened.

"That was a few days ago. Why are you just telling me? Marcus, that's very important. That's not something you keep away from your fiancé." I now realize that I just made a mistake. I've just opened her mind to wonder what else am I holding from her. Now she may become suspicious, and has every right to. "How did that conversation go? How did he know your mom was in the hospital?" I took a deep breath.

"I haven't begun to process that day, if we're being honest. I've tried to avoid thinking about it. Once I do process that day correctly I'll tell you about it. I wish you would have been there with me." Her eyes are getting watery.

"Here you go trying to make me feel bad. You are correct, I should have been there. I should have risked everything, including my job, and ran to the hospital to be by your side. I can always do better as a friend and significant other." I wiped the tears from her face.

"Don't feel bad, Tiffany. That wasn't my intention. Everything is happening so fast and I'm trying to get a grip on it. Just know that I love you and hope you'll always be by my side." I leaned over and kissed her. The waitress arrived with our food. She's a life saver. She's just rescued me from a conversation I'd rather not have.

Chapter 4

Dear Diary,

My dad wants back into my life. Excuse my language when I say fuck no. I haven't forgiven him, I don't want to forgive him. I'm not in denial about it. He's the blame for everything. I put all the blame on him. Is that fair? Probably not, but what if it's the truth? In my opinion, he did the unforgivable. He ruined the family as a whole. He ruined my mom and I on an emotional level. My mom is on her deathbed because of him. How does a woman accept closure in that situation? I've been trying to think of answers, but none have come back other than to just accept it. Easier said than done when you have emotions involved. What if my mom dies? What if she doesn't wake up out of the coma? It will be his fault. I'll pass on reconnecting with him. I've made it this far without him. Do I have a million questions I want to ask? Of course I do. I'll just keep the questions where they've been buried, a place in my heart. It's amazing the type of feelings a person can walk around with on the inside. The sad part is you'll never know. I now feel like everyone wears a mask. You'll never truly know a person. You're only loving or hating what you THINK you know about a person. A person could pour their soul out to you and still not tell you everything. I think that may be the cause of lots of suicides. Not being able to take off the mask and really be you. The real you may not be as loveable as the mask, and that sucks. I'm starting to think life isn't real. Life is just a spoof. I've written off the main subject. My dad, fuck him. Stay away from me. Stay with that individual you decided to choose over your family. I'll be fine. I rather sleep on all the unanswered questions I've been asking myself since I was a kid. "Does he love that man more than his son?" I now feel myself getting sad. No time for being sad. I have to be strong for my mom. I have to be strong for Tiffany, who loves my mom like she's her mom. Tiffany is crushed. I can't be around Tiffany like I should be because I cope better with liquor. The liquor handles my feelings easier and quicker, whatever that means. Then there's Camille....

Marcus

"Mom, I know you can't hear me. Well, I hope you can't hear me. If you wake up and remember this, I'm going to deny it all." I laughed. "I just want to tell you that I love you. My thoughts in my mind have been beyond crazy ever since you've been in this coma. One day I even thought to google how to put myself into a coma. I figured if you die, I want to die too, right beside you. I've always told myself I'd rather die before you. I'd make sure to watch over you from heaven. Now here we are. I'm not giving up on you, but already have cases of liquor if fate happens. Marcus is back around. Or should I say 'dad.' Him hearing about you in a coma all of a sudden brought him to the conclusion that he misses us. Fuck him. He's the reason you're in here. Mom, I'll never forgive him. Never."

"Is everything okay in here?" The doctor came in and looked at Mom. I nodded my head. What a dumb question to ask. My mom isn't awake yet. How can everything be okay? The doctor walked back out.

"Mom, I just can't figure out why God put you in this position. The first thing I thought is karma, but who have you done bad to? You're a kind-hearted woman. You've never been the type to lash your inner pain onto others. You just hold it all in. Why are you going through this? Ok, you like liquor and beer, so what? Plenty of people are the same way, including myself. Why am I not in this hospital bed instead of you? I'm a liar, a cheater, and an all-around horrible person. I'm basically a walking liar. My relationship is a lie. How am I going to marry a person who doesn't know that I have a drinking problem? I'm only marrying her to cover my reality of being in love with a….. another woman. I should be in a coma right now. If that was the case, then at least I wouldn't have to deal with reality. I'd hope to die so all my problems could go away. Mom, life is hard, and is only getting harder. Please, don't leave me, I'm begging you." I feel the tears starting to form in my eyes, which means I should get out of here.

I'm not sure if there's a more depressing place to be than the hospital. The place smells like death to me. I know they help people, but it's still depressing. It seems like they want to keep you alive for a while so they can take your money in the process. After they take enough of your money they let you die. Ok, I'll admit that I'm depressed and may not be thinking correctly. It seems like so much is going on at once. I need to sit down and figure everything out.

My home doesn't feel like home for some reason. The energy here feels different. No one has been over here but me, so it means I'm bringing bad energy here from the outside. I'm usually conscious of energy. I used to have a rule to never bring bad energy into my home. If I was ever angry or upset I'd wait outside until I was cool and happy again. I guess things have changed. Where is my pen and tablet?

Dear Diary,

My dad has another son. How? Yes, I know he and his significant other adopted him, but still I ask, how? What goes through a person's mind to make them think that would be a good idea? Now you want to come back into my life? The son you neglected, how? Am I insane for having these thoughts? You neglect your son and then go adopt a new son! Am I supposed to be okay with that? How do you leave me for another man, then adopt another boy? HOW? Someone help me understand. I should have bought a beer before starting this writing. I tried to open my heart and let him back in. This is what I get in return? How? His son looks like he's about eight. That's eight years that could have been spent getting to know me. No, I don't want to get to know him. Hell no! This book's words are stuck in my head. "Don't be afraid to express your feelings." Ok, I'm hurt. I take that back. I'm not hurt, I'm crushed. I have that same feeling I had the day he left me. Is this a permanent feeling? I'm going to get a drink before I lose my mind, if it isn't already lost.

Marcus

I'm fighting the urge to drink. Why? I guess this is my form of self-torture. Why does drinking have to be looked at as a bad thing? Ok, so it may do a little damage, that's not the point. Almost everything we do is hurting us if we're really being honest with ourselves. Most of the food we eat is killing us. No one is telling us to stop eating. I need a good distraction, a distraction that won't harm me, but will help me not think about life. I need a new escape.

My new escape can be Christina. I can spend time getting to know her again. Well, maybe that won't be a good idea. Christina has a way of making you think about yourself. I honestly miss Camille. She's altered my life in a negative way, but I still miss her. I wish she would stop playing the joke on me. It would put my heart at ease. My phone is ringing. I guess I've thought her into existence. I'm not going to answer it. Talking to her is not helping me get my life in order, though I don't know where to start in this process.

I somehow went from not answering the phone call to ending up in Camille's room, naked, with her on top of me. What is wrong with me? I used to think I was a strong-minded person. Maybe I've been lying to myself. Maybe I am strong-minded, maybe everyone has that one thing that gets to them. Mine happens to be her.

"I love you, daddy," Camille said as she got off me.

"Please, don't call me that," I blurted out. I didn't mean to say that. It was my first thought. We both have father issues, why would she call me that? Hearing her call me that made me cringe. I'm now upset and want to be away from her. The whole vibe has been ruined. What am I doing here?

"I'm sorry," she sadly stated. Now my dad is on my mind. Great, this is just what I need right now. "Why wouldn't you mind me calling you daddy? I thought you would like it?"

"I'm going to leave now." I got out the bed. Staying here will be good for no one. Don't call me daddy. I refer to my own dad by his first name, which is the same as mine. Why did they choose to name me that? Maybe I've been cursed since birth. I don't even have any kids to call me daddy. I'm extremely annoyed now. I should never come back.

I'm now driving, and still find myself annoyed. Why would she call me that? Am I making a big deal of nothing? Probably so, but that's not the point. We both have unresolved issues that we refuse to fix, but somehow have fell in love with each other. What does that say about us? I knew I shouldn't have gone over there.

I guess this is the downfall of cheating, you automatically compare the two. Tiffany is an emotionally secure individual. She comes to me for comfort, but absolutely hates having lingering, unresolved issues that will negatively affect her on an emotional level. She's really big on being happy. If anyone is doing something that will affect her happiness, she's always going to tell you in the proper manner. She likes to talk things out and get back on the same page. I love that about her.

I just received a text. It's Tiffany telling me to meet her at the park in fifteen minutes. She wants to have a picnic with me. Well isn't this wonderful. I now have to head to see my fiancé with another person's scent on me. Is my luck really this bad? How do I even pull this off while keeping a smile on my face? I feel guilt coming over me already. This may be a sign that I'm not heartless yet.

Tiffany has a way of soothing my soul. These types of things are things that make me happy. Beautiful weather, being outside, surrounded by people but focused on the individual in front of you. There's no money being spent, no ulterior motives, just pureness, a person wanting to bond. No fancy meals, just sandwiches and chips, but when you stare into the person's eyes, you can see the love.

"I just realized you didn't give me a hug," Tiffany said as she took a bite from her sandwich. I even like the white and red striped picnic blanket she chose. How can you damage someone who treats you so good? So many thoughts are going through my head.

"No, you didn't give me a hug," I said with a smile. "My feelings were hurt, I just chose not to say anything." She smiled and looked away. "Look at you, slowly falling out of love with me."

"I never fell in love with you from the beginning," she started. "I stood into love. There's a significant difference." Here she goes, pulling me in with her thoughts while also drowning me with guilt. "I decided to love you. I felt the feeling, but had to decide if I wanted to act on it. I took time to think on that decision. I weighed out the pros and cons of allowing such a powerful feeling to overtake me."

"I don't know what to say," I truthfully said.

"There's nothing you can say. These are my feelings. A con to the situation was that my feelings may always be stronger than yours. I accepted it, telling myself you would never hurt me, so my feelings would ultimately be secure. I may always love you more, and that's fine because I love hard, and really don't expect a person to love on my type of level. I just ask that you never hurt me. If you're ever unhappy, just leave."

"I've never hurt you, and I never will. I'm never leaving. You've given me no reasons to ever think about leaving." She smiled and nodded her head in agreement. This would usually be when I lean over and kiss her, but I have Camille's scent on me. I just looked Tiffany directly in the eye and lied to her. Why does God allow people like me to continue to live? I have my dad's lying tendencies.

****

"So, you weren't going to tell me your mom was in the hospital?" Christina asked.

"Who told you?"

"You know she's like my second mom. I even refer to her as mom to my own mom. It crushed my heart to hear that she's in a coma."

"Which is why I didn't tell you. You have your own problems." She sucked her teeth.

"I don't have any problems. I'm perfectly fine."

"If you say so."

"I saw your mistress in my dream." My eyes just widened.

"And you say you're perfectly fine?" I laughed. "Your actions and dreams tell me otherwise. How do you see someone who doesn't exist?" My friend is self-destructing in front of my eyes. I want to help, but don't know how. I think I'm in the process of accepting it, if that's even possible.

"If I knew who your girlfriend was, I would tell her." My eyes widened again.

"Why in the hell would you do that? Hypothetically speaking."

"Because you're not a cheater! I can't understand why you're doing it! I've been trying to figure it out. Since kids you've never been the one who wanted two girlfriends. You were always big on bonding with me. I don't know if the beer played a role in that, or it was genuinely you, but I know for sure you've been a one lady type of dude until now."

"Christina, what are you talking about? I was the quietest kid in school. I don't think I had a girlfriend until high school." Christina shook her head.

"No, you had girlfriends through the school years. You were probably too drunk to remember them. Wow, it's like….. I can't explain it. You have no memory of your school years."

"I can barely tell you any type of shoes or clothes I owned as a kid. I do remember doing homework a few times after school, or at least attempting to. How did I manage to graduate? I may naturally be smart. I can name all forty-five presidents right now, but can't tell you when or how I learned them."

"So, when are you taking me to the hospital to see your mom?" Christina asked.

"I'm not. I don't like being there. I'll give you the address if you want to go see her." Christina rolled her eyes.

"Marcus, it's your mom. She needs for you to be there!"

"I have been there. I've talked to her. If it's possible, she's heard my voice. I hate seeing her like that. When she wakes out the coma I'll be the first one there. Hopefully she wakes up sooner than later. Don't worry about going to see her. She will be up soon.

****

I opened my eyes. I feel Tiffany's head lying on my chest. I usually love sleeping like this, but not lately. I just woke up from dreaming about Camille. Why is she in my dreams while I'm sleeping with my fiancé? In the dream we were making love while the rain fell loudly outside. Great, it's actually raining now, but not as hard as it was in my dream. What does it all mean? What are the purposes of dreams? It's too early to have so many thoughts running through my head. It's 4:18 to be exact. I'm up before five, at my fiancé's home, thinking about another woman. I've never pictured myself being a cheater, but no one could've told me it would be like this.

I'll never understand how people cheat on their significant other with multiple people. This is very stressful. It may be because I actually wasn't unhappy, and didn't intend on cheating, though I'm unhappy now. Everything was going good. I'm the one that let…..curiosity ruin everything. Now look at me, unhappy with a great person I've been with for years because I'm now in love with someone I shouldn't even know.

I feel Tiffany's hand moving down to my midsection. I'm immediately erect now. She lifted her head, got on top of me, and quickly slid my dick inside of her. She's very warm. She put one finger over my lips and her other hand onto my chest. I grabbed her waist as she started to ride me. A gorgeous woman, even when she wakes up. I love that she doesn't wear makeup, just natural beauty.

She loves looking me directly into my eyes while she's on top, as if she's trying to read my thoughts and soul. I closed my eyes. It's not safe to read me right now. She sped up her movements. She's moaning loudly, I'm breathing hard. I roughly pulled her more into me. I feel all of me coming inside of her. Wow, I came hard. She leaned over and placed her head on my chest, without getting off me. I'm still inside of her, my eyes are still closed. This is how we will fall asleep, hopefully until sunrise.

"I want to start off by apologizing," he said.

"You're cool," I calmly replied. I don't know why I agreed to this. I'm a mixture of emotions at the moment. Hate, sadness, nervousness, excitement, mostly hate though. My face shows no emotion. I'm actually sitting across from my dad while at Starbucks. This is my first time spending time with him in about eighteen years. I look nothing like him. I'm a spitting image of my mother in the face, which is fine with me. At least I know she cares.

"So, how have you been?" he asked with a smile.

"I've been good."

"Do you want to fill in the blanks for me? Catch me up on all the years I've missed?"

"Not really," I bluntly replied. He took a sip of his coffee.

"I guess I should have expected that answer."

"Cool."

"So, you're going to give me these short responses the entire time?"

"Pretty much."

"Maybe this wasn't a good idea. Maybe the imagination of us working things out was crazy of me for even thinking." He stood up. "It was nice seeing you, son."

"OK, Marcus." He walked away. *Inhale slowly, exhale slowly.* The emotions that are running through my body are indescribable. I really want to breakdown and cry.

"How was it?" Camille asked. She's giving me a back massage. I never knew this, but a back massage has to be my weakness. Soft hands touching my back…..it does something to me.

"I wanted to cry," I truthfully replied. "It took everything inside of me to not break down and cry right in front of him."

"I'm sorry baby."

"It's fine. It was just too much to take in. It was way more to intake than I expected."

"Will you see him again?"

"Fuck him. I rather stay walking around with the pain on the inside."

"Baby, pain isn't a good thing to walk around with."

"I've been walking around with it for this long and haven't died yet. A little while longer won't hurt me. If only he knew how much I was burning on the inside. There's so many questions...." I can't even finish my sentence. I just remembered that Camille doesn't know the story about my dad. Wow, I can't even talk to her about it. The connection between them might make things....weird. Now, suddenly I feel weird.

"Baby, you stopped speaking." I'm really speechless. What am I supposed to say? I am my dad. I'm doing the exact same thing. My mom did nothing wrong to him, Tiffany has done no wrong to me. I need my therapist. Living in my mind isn't good for me. The person I should be talking to, I can't because I'm cheating on her. I can't talk to my mom, she's in a coma. She would be devastated. Like father, like son, almost literally. I turned onto my back, now looking upwards at Camille.

"Get on top of me," I seductively said. She smiled, pulled her shorts and panties off, and got on top of me. I have no beer, so I'll just sex my problems away.

"I think I'm addicted to you," Camille said as she put her head on my chest, the same spot where Tiffany places her head. The sex we have is beautiful. "Your personality, your scent, your knowledge, the way your mind seems to work. It's all addicting. I could spend every moment with you if it was possible. I feel like we're on the same rhythm. Sometimes, while you sleep, I just lie on your chest and listen to your heartbeat. You seem at peace when you sleep with me. There's no snoring, no tossing and turning, just peaceful sleeping."

"That's nice to know."

"I've saved you a drawer and space in my closet that you've never walked into. No, I'm not rushing you, but if you ever want the space, it's yours. I'm yours." Reality is sinking in quickly.

****

I hung up the phone. Wow, she's really dead. *Marcus, just breathe.* My mom is dead. Four days ago, I told Christina she'd be up soon. Does that make me a liar? Wow, my mom really is gone. I'm repeating it to make sure I'm processing the information correctly. My mom is dead. Shit, how did that happen? I can't explain how I'm feeling right now. I think…..I think I'm shocked. My phone is ringing. My mom, my best friend, my everything, she's dead. I'm going to go to sleep now.

Dear Diary,

3:56am with a bottle of liquor in my hand. Mom died, like, she really died. I'm accepting it the only way I know how to accept things. That's with the liquor. I'm already drunk, but not drunk enough. I want to blackout and never wake up. Fuck life. I'm not going back to work. Fuck a job. To take it to the extreme, I'm never leaving this apartment again. I have enough beer and liquor to last me a few months. I'm just going to drink, pass out, wake up, and repeat the cycle. I haven't cried, I haven't returned any phone calls. I just want to be with the beer and liquor. I need to write my death note to Tiffany. I'm not going to apologize to her, I'm just going to tell her that I love her, but love a man, that's now a woman, who looks better than her, a little more. Ok, I love Camille a lot more. Fuck it, I'm in full acceptance mode now. I love a man. I love the soul of a man, and I'm tired of denying it. A man has stolen my heart from a woman. I can't leave this man alone. I've been lying to myself, telling myself all types of excuses that what I'm doing isn't really wrong. Camille's not a man. She's a woman. She's just playing a joke. Or, she just wasn't done evolving yet. She was meant to be a woman. A man could never make another man feel so good and pure. I'M MY DAD! Marcus, I now understand you, without actually understanding you. That's because it can't be understood. I get it now. You have to be in the person's shoes.

Judging from the outside is stupid. You can't control how you feel about a person. You can't control which soul you connect with. Me and Marcus just happened to connect with men. Shit happens, it's just a part of life. I think I killed my mom. I think she heard everything I told her while I was at the hospital. She couldn't accept it. It would be too much to handle if she was to wake up, so she just decided to die, and it's all my fault. I'm a walking fuck-up. I'm a walking disaster. A disaster happens with everyone I come in contact with. Mom is dead, Christina is mentally damaged, Tiffany is on the receiving end of the consequences of being a great significant other. And Camille, HE is also mentally damaged. Him and I are made for each other. We both need psychological help. Tiffany deserves better, and will get better. I'm not leaving this apartment until the ambulance takes me out. I will write Tiffany's letter next, making sure I tell her everything. Maybe I won't write her. I have more liquor waiting in this attempt to permanently clear my mind.

Marcus

Someone is knocking hard on my door. I'm laid on my living room floor. My mind is telling me to get up, but my body won't agree. My head is throbbing. I feel like I'm glued to the floor. I have a massive headache. I can barely open my eyes.

"Marcus, open up!" The knocking is continuing. I can't understand whose voice it is. It may be Tiffany's, it may be Camille's, it may be Christina's, it may be Mom's. None of their voices sound alike. My mind just can't process the voice. I still have a bottle of whiskey in my hand that's almost empty. I feel that the top is on the bottle, which is a good thing, otherwise the whiskey would be all over me or on the floor. That wouldn't be good. The knocking is giving me a headache. Can't you understand that I'm not here!

"Open the door, Marcus!" I opened the bottle of whiskey and drank the rest. Well, that was quite tasty. My blinds are closed, but I can still see the sun shining. What time is it? It doesn't matter, I'm going back to sleep.

I opened my eyes. I feel that the side of my face is wet. Great, I'm sleeping in my own puke. I don't remember puking. I was hoping it was just slob, but I know I don't slob when I'm sleep. I grabbed a can of beer from nearby. When am I going to get up from this spot? Never! Why am I not dead yet? I know that I stink. I can smell the odor, oh well. Beer really doesn't have a taste anymore, which may be a strong sign that I have a problem. It tastes like water.

My body is aching. Shit, I'm in the process of mourning, my body should ache. This shouldn't be unusual. Drink the pain away. That sounds like a great idea. I feel myself wanting to puke. I'm a strong man, I will not give in. I WILL NOT PUKE! *Stay strong, Marcus.* I picked up another can of beer. I'm in so much pain that I can barely lift myself up to drink the beer. I've never felt this type of body pain before. Fuck it, let's see how much pain my body can tolerate. The body has a way of getting immune to things.

****

The funeral is starting while I'm here in my car with a bottle of Hennessy. This is what Mom liked to drink, so this is what I'll drink, directly across the street from where the funeral is happening. This is the closes I'll be towards seeing my mom in a casket. Is it selfish? Maybe, but I can't do it. I refuse to let my last memory of my mom be in a casket. My last memory of her will be in the hospital, but at least I can say she was alive. It's a lot of cars outside of the church. I never knew Mom knew so many people.

I probably should go in there now, but know that would be an idiotic decision considering I'm drunk right now. I can feel it. I have two more bottles on the passenger seat. I think I went through the first bottle too fast. Something is telling me to walk in there. I'm fighting the urge. What would happen if I went up to the casket? I'd probably lose my mind, literally. I can't risk the embarrassment to my mom. She's probably sad that I'm not at her funeral. I hope she knows I'm truly sorry.

I opened my eyes. There's a knock on the window. I can feel the beam of the flashlight. Is that the police? Shit, I've fallen asleep in the car. I'm about to go to jail for drinking and driving. Well, I technically wasn't driving, I'm sitting. The knocking is continuing. My head is turned so he can't tell if my eyes are open or not. At this point, I really don't care. Maybe jail is the best place for me to be. I turned around. I can't see the face because of the glare from the flash light. I let down the window.

"Are you okay?" he asked as he turned off the flashlight. Well, it's not a cop. Judging by the suit, I'd have to guess it being a pastor. Great, I'd rather it be a cop. At least I'd know what I'm dealing with.

"Yes, I'm fine," I said while wiping my eyes. "I'd grown tired while driving. I didn't want to risk falling asleep on the road so I pulled over."

"Is that right?" He pointed to the bottles. Great, I was hoping he wouldn't see those. Now what am I supposed to say? I've already lied to him once.

"Hey, I'm not hurting anyone, and I wasn't drinking while driving. No, I'm not homeless. I'd just like to be left alone." I wonder what time is it. How long was I sleeping? The pastor nodded his head and walked across the street, back into the church. Well, it's night time now, which means I've been sleeping for hours. Now I must avoid everyone.

Well, speaking of avoiding everyone, I see I have forty-eight missed calls. It's probably forty-eight people wanting to know why I didn't attend the funeral. Tiffany is probably included in those people. I didn't even think about her before making my decision. I'm going to have to explain myself. I can't avoid her forever. Vanishing for a while seems like a great idea right now. Let me figure out a way to get my life in order, if that's even possible.

****

I've been living in a small motel for a week. I couldn't go to my place because I know that's where I could be found. I've just wanted to be away from everyone and everything. I haven't had any liquor and very little food. I've just wanted to be alone with me and my thoughts.

It's safe to say this past week has been a week of torture. I've always proclaimed me as a person who doesn't mind being alone, a person that doesn't need to be around a lot of people. I now know that I have no problem being alone WITH liquor. I've technically never been alone before. My loneliness void has been filled with cups and bottles. Being alone is quite scary.

I've decided to leave the liquor alone. I want to spend time with me. I've always had a scapegoat. Maybe there is nothing wrong with having a scapegoat. Maybe having a scapegoat is better than relying on yourself. I don't know, I'm just thinking clearly for the first time in a long time. I've attempted to stop drinking before but would sneak in a cup occasionally. It's time to go deal with the real world now. This week has been a learning experience.

Well, isn't this a surprise. Tiffany's car is parked at my apartment. She doesn't have a key, so she must be inside of it. How long has she been here? I wanted to get my reasoning for disappearing sorted out over a hot shower. My disappearance was a bad idea, now that I think about it. I've given myself too much time to think and that's never a good thing. She quickly got out her car. Maybe I should stay in mine.

"Are you going to let down the window?" she asked as she reached my car door. She doesn't look happy. She looks like she's achieved very few hours of sleep. I now feel guilty, like an arrogant piece of shit. That's maybe too harsh to label myself as, but it may be true. The bottles of liquor are still on my seat and I have nothing to cover them. I quickly got out and closed my door.

"Tiffany," I started, "What are you doing here?" Her expression shows she's thinking about slapping me. I guess that was a stupid question, but I don't know what else to ask. It's actually cold out here today. I still have on my clothes from a week ago. I know I stink, I have to.

"Marcus, where have you been?" she sadly asked. "I haven't slept in three days and have been waiting outside your apartment for two days with no food." Tears are starting to form in her eyes. "What's going on?"

"Let's get inside. We both could use some food and a shower." I walked to my apartment and opened the door. It's colder in here than it is outside. I guess that would be the case when you've had no electricity flowing through for a week. I turned on the heater and walked into my room. I pointed towards the drawer where I keep Tiffany's clothes and underwear. I quickly took off my clothes, walked into the bathroom, turned on the water and got in. Tiffany followed me into the shower.

We probably should be talking right now, but the hot water probably feels better to the both of us. This is a moment where I wish I could read minds. If I could read her mind, I then would know what to say. She must have a million questions running through her head. Who is going to ask a question first? It should probably be me, but I don't know what to ask. I should make a sexual move on her to hopefully make her forget. Sex always has a way of reminding a person that emotions are involved between the two, even if it's temporarily. Unfortunately, Tiffany is smarter than most. It's always a thinking game with her.

"So, are we going to talk?" she asked as we put on our clothes. I honestly don't know where to start. I don't know what to even say. My lack of response is putting worry on her face. "I'm waiting, Marcus."

"What would you like to know?" I asked. She has that expression of wanting to slap me again. She took a deep breath. I hate when she takes deep breaths.

"Why didn't you attend the funeral? Where have you been for the past week? Those are two questions I'd like answered."

"I couldn't make it to the funeral."

"Marcus, what do you mean you couldn't make it to the funeral? It's your mother for God's sake!"

"I just couldn't do it. Any reason I give you may not be good enough. I just couldn't do it. I couldn't see my mom dead. I haven't been to church in years. I wasn't going to let my first time in years be for a funeral."

"Marcus, that's a dumb answer. It's your mom's funeral!"

"I told you I had no good reasons. Those are my reasons though."

"You left me there alone, answering all the questions. Everyone's asking where are you, and me having no answers. I couldn't even lie my way out of those questions, and I absolutely hate lying. I didn't know where you were at, which is what I told them. It was the most awkward thing ever. I've never been so embarrassed in my life!"

"I'm sorry."

"You're sorry? Is that all you have to say? Marcus, that's not enough. I need answers!"

"Answers to what!"

"What is wrong with you?" In my opinion, she's asking the question she doesn't want the answer to. What's wrong with me? Everything is wrong with me. She's in love with a person she barely knows. I don't even know me anymore. To be honest, I don't think I've ever known me. How can a person know themselves when they barely have a memory? I only have more memories because my liquor intake has decreased. It's no longer a daily thing. From the ages of ten to nineteen I was drinking every day. I was drinking beer and liquor like water. Honestly, I think I've had more liquor than water. Why aren't I dead?

"Tiffany, nothing is wrong with me. My mom is dead and I don't know how to deal with it. My best friend is gone. Have you ever permanently lost a best friend? Excuse me for being confused with life!" I walked into the living room. Camille just came to my mind. She's just a reminder of the double, I mean triple life I'm living. She doesn't even know my mom is dead. She knew she was in the hospital, but not in a coma. How did I get to this point in life? This is not how I had it planned.

"I'm sorry," Tiffany said as she reached the living room. "I guess I got stuck in only seeing things from my point of view. Looking at things from your point of view, I guess I understand a little better. That doesn't mean I agree with your actions. We're supposed to be a team. You could have sent me a text saying you're going ghost to get your mind right."

"Would you have accepted that text message without an explanation?" I asked.

"To accept something and understand something is two different actions. This is a tough time for you. It's very critical that I'm being an understanding partner right now. That comes from communication. I'm not inside your brain, though I wish I could be. I can't read your thoughts. For understanding on my end, you have to put me in a position to understand. Am I asking for too much? Please, tell me if I am."

"You're not asking for too much. I'm sorry for the lack of communication." I hugged her. There's much more I should be apologizing to her for.

"Marcus, where have you been?" Camille asked. "I've been calling you for a week. I've missed you dearly. A week without talking to you seems like years."

"I was finding myself," I bluntly replied.

"What does that mean?" she asked back. What's up with all these questions? I feel like I'm going through hours of interrogation. Is it bad for me to want a few days to myself? I don't feel like I'm asking for much. I'm not telling Camille my mom died, though I badly want to. I don't feel like going through the sadness. I just want to…..I don't know what I want anymore.

"I just needed a few days to get my thoughts together. Sometimes we all need silence so we can be alone with our thoughts. I could have done a better job in telling you I'm going into silence. I truly apologize."

"Were any of those thoughts about me?" she happily asked. I'm just realizing that for a full week Camille didn't get a thought. No one really got a thought outside of my mom. It's actually hard to explain my thoughts during that week. It was like I was wrestling with demons. There weren't any happy thoughts.

"Of course I thought about you. I'm always thinking about you." I kissed her on the lips. Why do lies sound so much better than the truth? Why do lies feel better than the truth? I guess it's a fact that reality is ugly, and it's not fair. Why are lies more beautiful? Doesn't that make life backwards? Maybe my thoughts are just wrong.

"You should have taken me with you. There would have been no need for words. I just like being in your presence. You could have been on the other side of the room in deep thought. I would have been happy to just be there."

"Sometimes it's good to be alone in a dark room. Have no phone, no laptop, no music, just yourself in that moment. Sit there and spend time with your thoughts."

"I think that would scare me," Camille admitted. "I guess I've become too reliant on technology and music. I think I would go crazy without them. Wow, you just made me realize how much of a distraction they are and how addicted I am to them. Wow, music and technology are my legal drugs. Shit, I really do have a problem."

"Have you ever tried any drugs?" I asked.

"Weed used to be my escape, though I don't consider that a drug. I used to smoke three blunts a day. Weed kept me away from the bullshit that had its way of coming into my life, at least mentally. It kept my stress levels down. Then you came into my life. Once you came into my life, I don't know why, but the urge to smoke suddenly stopped. Even when we go through our problems, I still don't run back to it. You're in my life for a reason."

"Maybe the reason will be revealed to us one day. I think about it occasionally. Is there no such thing as an accident? Do you really come across each person for a specific reason? I'm still trying to figure out why I've met certain people throughout life. Sometimes I think I meet a lot of people to learn what not to do."

"Would that mean you think you're right more times than you're not?" Camille asked. I just thought of Christina and her calling me a narcissist. "This is off topic, but do you think we will ever stay the night together?"

"Whoa, where did that question come from? I wasn't expecting that one." She looked away. Part of me wants an answer, but the greater part of me doesn't. I've never thought of us living together. I've never thought of waking up with her. Is that crazy of me? All I've thought of are experiencing good moments with her, I guess my version of good moments. I guess I am suffering from wanting everything to be my way, but don't we all? Even when I planned on leaving Tiffany, my thoughts on what happens afterwards weren't clear.

"Forget that I asked," she sadly said. I know she's effected by my answer. She must understand that I'm new to this whole idea of cheating. I've been in sync with one person for years without any distractions until recently. Being in sync was also going well. I feel myself getting upset. I've ruined everything. How do I ruin a good situation? Now I feel like I'm in too deep to get out. I should call my dad and ask him how did he do it. We're basically the same person. Yes, I've officially made myself mad, even pissed-off, even if it's at myself. I need someone else to blame.

It's now night time. I'm drinking while driving. I know this is wrong but will think about the consequences later. I'm on the way to Misha's apartment. This is her fault, all of it. She brought Camille around me. She must know that Camille is a man. Why would you leave her…..him around me? Why ruin my life. I can feel the liquor having an effect on me. If I choke Misha out, we will just blame it on the liquor.

My body is filled with rage. I probably should pull over and cry. Mom's dead, I can't turn off my feelings for Camille, I hate that Tiffany genuinely loves me, and I have no one to talk to. Do I really feel this way? Or is it just the liquor? Maybe I really feel this way. I'm the one that claims I've been drinking so long that liquor does nothing to me. Maybe that's a lie too. My life has turned into a lie.

I feel my vision getting blurry. That's a good thing. If I happen to strangle Misha, I can argue that I could barely see her. I hope her son isn't here. I don't want him to see me go ballistic on his mom. Well, it may be a good thing if he is here. How I'm feeling right now, I literally want to kill.......

****

I hear a beeping noise. I opened my eyes. Am I dreaming? Where am I? I looked to my right. I'm hooked up to a machine. I'm in a hospital, but how? I leaned up, I see Tiffany and two cops. What are the cops doing here? Fear is in my heart. What did I do? Tiffany's eyes widened as she glanced at me.

"He's alive!" She quickly walked towards me and kissed me on the lips. "Baby, you were in a car crash. Oh my God, they found bottles of liquor in the car. Baby, why were you drinking? Is everything okay? You were extremely over the alcohol limit. Baby, talk to me."

"May we ask you a few questions?" One of the cops asked as they both reached my bed.

"No, you may not ask him any questions!" Tiffany angrily replied. "He just awoke, let him get his thoughts together." She turned back to me. "Baby, talk to me. Tell me what's wrong."

"Oh my God." Fear just leaped into my heart. Oh my God, that's Camille's voice! Tiffany and I's glances quickly switched to the door. It's her, it's really her. What is she doing here? Who told her I was here? I just found out I was here! Hold on, how long have I been here? I need to sort my thoughts out. Things are happening too fast. I haven't spoken a word yet.

"Who are you?" Tiffany asked. Oh shit. I don't know what to do or say.

"I'm Camille," she replied as she extended her hand. "You must be Tiffany."

"I am. Who are you?"

"I'm Marcus' supervisor. He's told me a lot about you. He even has pictures of you at his cubicle." Is Camille crazy? I have nothing at my cubicle but a computer and phone! Thank God Tiffany has never been inside my job. Now I have to make sure she never comes in. Tiffany has a great memory, she will remember this.

"Marcus, you never told me you have such a beautiful supervisor. I never knew your supervisor was a woman." She shook Camille's hand.

"Marcus, you were on the news. They spoke on your car accident and had received your name. As soon as I heard the name I rushed here. You're my top worker, I can't lose you." I'm almost positive that Camille doesn't know what I do for work. If Tiffany gets to asking her questions, then I'm screwed. Why would she come here? "I'm happy you're alive. The accident looked bad."

"We need to ask you a few questions," the same cop said.

"Eight different opened bottles of liquor were found in your car," the other cop said.

"Eight different bottles?" Tiffany asked.

"Marcus, were you trying to kill yourself?" Camille asked.

"When in the hell did you start drinking?" You can hear the anger in Tiffany's voice, which is scary because Tiffany rarely gets angry.

"Marcus, what's going on?" Camille asked.

"May you please explain the bottles?" The first cop asked.

"Where were you headed?" The other cop asked.

"Marcus, do you have a drinking problem?" Camille asked.

"Marcus, help me understand!" Tiffany sadly pleaded. I'm going to close my eyes and go back to sleep. I'm sure this is one horrible nightmare. I'll wake up to find myself in the bed with Tiffany.

Chapter 5

So much for waking up realizing it's all a nightmare. I'm in county jail now. How did I get to this point? I'm sure I will get bailed out soon, but that's not the point. I'm really in jail. I actually told Tiffany to let me stay in here for a few days to clear my head. I definitely have some explaining to do once I get out, and want to avoid that explaining, so I may stay in here forever. There's no expectations or pressure in here. There's just me and my thoughts. I really miss my mom.

"Are you okay?" Tiffany asked as I got into her blue Toyota Camry. After spending three days in there, I'm not even sure if that's enough. I was getting comfortable with the jail's scent. Now I'm back into the clean air. I went from the hospital to jail, so this is the first conversation Tiffany and I will really be having. She must have a ton of questions. I have a ton of questions for myself that I haven't answered.

"I'm fine. How are you, Tiffany? How's everything at work? What's going on in the news? Have we declared war on a new country yet?"

"Marcus, you were gone for three days, not three years." I laughed and nodded my head. "And everything has been fine. These three days have been lonely. Luckily Camille has been there to console me." I feel myself about to explode with anger. *Inhale slowly, exhale slowly.* Tiffany has lectured me on not acting on my initial emotion. I may be stubborn, but these are one of the few times I'm happy I listened.

"Well, that's nice," I calmly stated. "I didn't know the two of you were hanging out. I don't even hang out with her. I barely like her being my supervisor." I forced a laugh.

"She's been extremely helpful! She's a great listener, she gives great feedback. I was able to easily vent to her, and felt very comfortable while doing it. She seems to have a gift for understanding people. I don't know, it's weird. You know I don't open up to everyone. She just gives out a certain type of energy."

"That's nice to know." I seriously don't know what else to say. I don't consider myself to be an angry person, but to say that I'm extremely pissed would be an understatement. I need a drink, and yes, I know drinking is the reason for all of this. No, Camille is the reason for all of this. She has ruined my life, but I love her. How can you love someone who has ruined you?

"I think I want to start hanging with her more often," Tiffany happily said. *Marcus, just breathe.* "I think her and I can become great friends."

"I'm not even her friend," I stated. "We are co-workers. I'm not sure if I'm comfortable letting her into our lives."

"Well, she did come and check on you. That says a lot about her."

"She's my supervisor. That's what she's supposed to do." I feel myself getting annoyed.

"Hey, she doesn't have to be a part of our life. She can be part of my life. You have your friends, I have my friends. This is nothing different. What's your problem? Why do you seem so against me being friends with her?"

"It just seems odd. I wouldn't dare become friends with any of those weirdos at your job." She burst out laughing.

"Don't talk about my co-workers! They love me and I love them! Your job may be full of weirdos also. I've just never been inside to see. You must let me meet them one day." This is exactly what I feared. My heart is beating fast. Reacting in a negative way will raise questions. My life seems to be crumbling from every direction.

"If you love them, and they love you, that makes you a weirdo also." She punched me in my arm, while using her other hand to control the steering wheel. I need to keep the conversation going. I want to avoid the real conversation that hasn't happened yet. If I hadn't proposed already, I'd definitely use that moment for now. Wait, that's it! "Why you've been out here hanging with Camille, all I've been doing is thinking about the wedding." She's focused on the road, but I can tell that statement made her happy.

"What were your thoughts?" she calmly asked, clearly trying to hide her excitement.

"They were just focused on how I want that day to be completely focused on you. If a perfect day is possible, I want that day to be it. I want to be in the background. Any happiness I'm feeling will solely be based off your energy. I want to pause while everything is going on and be confident that the day is perfect to you, and it's the happiest you've ever been."

"I've never mentioned this, but Marcus, I've had many perfect days with you. I've always been scared to say it. It's funny, Camille and I were talking about this yesterday." Well, now I don't know what to say. The way I imagined this conversation going just took a left turn. What I planned on our wedding being is days I've already given her. I'm actually speechless. How do I reply to her statement? "You're quiet over there."

"I just momentarily got lost into my thoughts." We pulled up to her apartment. I really wish she would have dropped me off to my place. I want to be alone for a while. Space will probably have to be sacrificed once we're married. I deeply feel that's going to change me. I won't be able to be the same person. I like to be alone at times. I'm going to become unhappy. Well, I'm unhappy now, so I should get used to the feeling.

"We can talk now," Tiffany said as I closed the front door. She's smart, she knew what she was doing. She wanted to wait until she could look me in my eyes. The eyes never lie, which is why people like to wear shades. I hope my eyes can miraculously achieve the unachievable. We sat down on the black leather couch.

"What would you like to talk about?" I asked.

"Everything," she quickly replied.

"What's everything?" I didn't think about this conversation while in jail.

"That's what I should be asking you. Talk to me, what's going on? What are you keeping from me?" She's asking all the questions I have no answer to. I honestly don't know where or how to start. People call me a narcissist. Well, the narcissist is stuck. "Let's start with the drinking." I have no words. "Eight bottles of opened liquor? What caused you to buy that many bottles and have them opened?"

"I had an urge to try some liquor, so I went to the store to try some various kinds." She shook her head.

"Is that the best lie you can come up with, Marcus?"

"Well, I don't think it would be a good thing if I was a great liar." She squinted her eyes at me. "I can't explain why I had all of the liquor. I just did. I miss my mom and don't know how to deal with it." I'm really using the death of my mom as a scapegoat. My heart is in the right place, and my intentions are good.

"Marcus, I'm the person you come talk to about everything. When did running to liquor seem like the better option?" Do I finally tell her everything? This would be the perfect time, start over fresh. If she leaves, at least it will be before we got married and have to go through the divorce process. This is my time to stop the lies. Maybe this is the moment I've been waiting for. It's funny how I arrived here.

"Tiffany, you just don't understand."

"Baby, I want to understand." She touched my hand. "We're getting married, we have to work out these situations. Do you have a drinking problem that I don't know about?"

"Of course not. I don't even like the taste of it. I didn't feel like talking to anyone, so I tried talking to the liquor. I'm not a drinker, I couldn't expect the effects. When I started driving I was perfectly fine. I guess the effects hit me at once. I remember what song I was listening to before everything went black. It will never happen again. I'm happy to be alive. It's safe to say that liquor or beer isn't for me."

"Why do I feel like you're holding something back from me?" she asked. *Because your feeling is correct!*

"How about we speed up the process of getting a place together. I want you to see that I'm fine and am hiding nothing. We can even get an extra bedroom. I know you've been dying to turn a room into a mini library." She smiled and nodded her head.

"I also want a room for drawing and painting. Maybe we need a house." I smiled and winked. "Don't wink at me. That wink means you're thinking we also need an extra room for a future child. You and I both know you're not ready for kids. You just like to talk about it."

"Hey, you're making me sound like the woman in this relationship!" I smiled, leaned forward and kissed her. I have no clue what I'm doing. I'm just moving with the motions. I'm doing the exact thing I've been telling myself I'm scared to do. It is the only way out of the situation. I mean, I could always just leave, but that's not a real option anymore. I'm moving in with my fiancé, and my fiancé and side girl are now friends. And my side girl claims she's a transgender that's happily made her way into my personal life. How did I allow all of this to happen? I really wrote some horrible things that night I was drunk. I didn't mean any of it.

Some good came out of being in that accident. It was a good excuse for my real supervisor to give me my job back. I really had no plans of coming back, but since my life has shifted, I now have no choice. Wow, I was really ready to give up on life. I take that back, I had given up on life. I wanted to die on my living room floor. I was at peace with myself. Now I'm in a worse position than I was before I'd given up.

The job has been expressing their feelings to me today. I guess everyone heard about the accident. Supposedly, I totaled my car. I've been scared to look at any photos. I just take people's word for it. I've had two recent moments where I was supposed to die but didn't. What type of sign is God trying to send me? The only sign I'm seeing is a reminder of how unhappy I am. I'm going home now with the excuse that I'm feeling under the weather. I only came here to attempt to get my job back.

Looking around my apartment now makes me sad. I don't want to give it up. I don't want anything anymore. I don't want to get married, I don't want Camille, I don't want Tiffany. I just want to start over. I haven't talked to Camille since getting out of jail. I honestly don't know what to say to her. My thoughts have been so angry lately, and I'm not an angry person. I might just curse her out, and I'm not that type of person. I'm a very respectful man.

This may be the real sign from God. This may be his way of telling me to turn my feelings off for her. She crossed the line by coming to the hospital. Then you have the nerve to become friends with my fiancé? Aren't I supposed to be angry with her? The feelings won't leave and it really bothers me. I don't know if it's my heart or my mind that's damaging me. It may be both, and that's scary. When your heart and mind are on the same page, and you end up being wrong, what does that really say about the person? This is what happens when I think too much. I believe I have the ability to think myself crazy.

I opened a can of Budweiser. Here I am, back drinking, doing the same thing that almost killed me twice. I wish my mom was here. She would make me feel more comfortable and accept me. Someone is knocking on my door. Who could that be? It can't be Camille, she's never been here. Tiffany is at work. Maybe it's Christina. She's probably mad that I've been avoiding her, though not purposely. She probably heard about the accident. I looked through the peephole, it's Camille. I opened the door.

"Marcus," she softly said.

"What?"

"I'm so happy to see you. May I come in?" I now regret taking off my shirt before having a beer. I feel her looking at my bare chest and abs. Am I an alcoholic? Yes. There's nothing that 800 sit-ups a day won't keep under control. No beer belly for me.

"No, you may not come in."

"Marcus, why not?" My anger levels are rising. *Marcus, stay calm.* "I've missed you."

"Camille," I calmly started, "Are you mentally insane?" She has a look of confusion on her face.

"Of course not. Why would you ask me that? Where is this coming from?" I took a deep breath. I really want to scream right now. Where is all this rage coming from?

"Camille, you're at my apartment. I've never given you the address. You show up to the hospital before I even realize I'm in the hospital, while my fiancé is there. Camille, something in that brain of yours thought it would be a good idea to become friends with my fiancé."

"A fiancé you claim you don't love and don't want to be with," she shot back.

"Camille, that's not the point." I've never said I don't love Tiffany. This isn't the time to argue over that though.

"Well, Marcus, tell me what's the point? It's very rude of you to leave me in this hall when you can easily let me come in."

"Camille, please go home." I went to close the door. She stopped the door, using her hand.

"Marcus, why are you acting like this? What changed all of a sudden? I need to talk to you. I need to figure out what's wrong. What distorted thoughts are you having? Let me help you."

"You need to do that for yourself," I blurted out.

"What is that supposed to mean?"

"Nothing, I didn't mean it." I stepped to the side and let her come in. Acting on my thoughts has put me in a bad spot. Now I have her in my place, a place I had no plans of her seeing. Why does it feel like I'm losing control of everything? This isn't how life is supposed to go for me. I'm used to having things under control, planned in my favor.

"You have a nice spot," she said as she looked around. "It looks much better than I envisioned. You actually have taste." She sat on my couch.

"My fiancé has taste," I stated as I sat down. I hope she clearly hears the dissatisfaction in my voice. "How did you get my address? Are you stalking me?" She shook her head.

"Marcus, you're not about to paint me as a crazy woman. Tiffany, your fiancé, my friend, gave me your address."

"Your friend? You've only known her for three days. How in the hell is she your friend?" I'm trying to control my anger. I'm not sure if it's working or not.

"Well, Tiffany and I have seemed to connect quickly, just like you and I, in different ways of course," she smiled. Is it possible? Could her and Tiffany really be friends so soon? No, it's not possible. I know Tiffany, she's not that vulnerable to let a complete stranger get close to her. I don't care if she's supposed to be my supervisor. I feel myself becoming angry with everyone.

The knock on the door made both of us jump. I hope it's Tiffany. I want to get this situation cleared. I want to set the record straight that they can't be friends. I have to regain control of things. I opened the door. Shit, it's Christina. I should have looked through the peephole. "Christina," I said with a smile, "What brings you by?" She looked over my shoulder.

"That's her," she whispered.

"Huh?"

"That's the girl I saw in my dream. That's who you're cheating on Tiffany with. How dare you bring her to your place." How is this even possible? I thought the medicine was getting to Christina. She's right, and my facial expression can't hide it, though I'm trying to. I can't think of a lie quickly enough to get me out of this situation. "I'm going to leave now." She turned around and walked away.

"What was that about?" Camille asked as I closed the door. I quickly pulled down my gray sweatpants. Camille's eyes just lit up with amazement. She loves what she sees. I signaled her to my bedroom, the bedroom that no one has ever been in besides my fiancé. Even Mom never saw what my room looked like. This is supposed to be a place of love, securement, privacy, and everlasting memories. I'm about to ruin it all.

"Marcus, I love you." She's smiling as she looks up at the ceiling. I say nothing back. I honestly don't know what to say. My secret is out without telling anyone. Christina officially knows I'm a cheater. What if she has another dream and learns that Camille isn't lying about being a transgender? Great, now that thought is going to stay in my head.

"Let's run away," I said. Her head turned towards me.

"Why would we do that? Things have changed now. We just can't leave." I'm confused with her answer. I thought she would be excited to run away with me. I want to start over, change my name, grow my hair out, become a whole new person. I want to erase my past. I'd even give up liquor. I just want to be new, different.

"What has changed?"

"I have a new friend. I just can't leave her." My thoughts are racing. The smart action would be to accept defeat, to accept that I have no control over anything. But no, not me, I won't do it. You must have some type of control over your life. You're either controlling or being controlled, to a certain extent. If you're being controlled, then, well, you're just a robot, a robot with the illusion of having real thoughts and feelings.

"Whatever you say." I got out the bed. My room will never be the same, I can already feel it. The specialness to this room is now gone. I was supposed to be different, different from the rest of the men. Maybe I was just lying to myself.

****

"How do you choose between two amazing people?" I asked the therapist. I'm back lying on the couch while staring at the ceiling, still doing a great job in avoiding eye contact. I need to bring Tiffany and Camille here. Too bad neither know I'm going crazy on a mental level.

"Well, what makes the two of these individuals amazing? Are there differences or similarities?" I scratched my head.

"You know what? I really don't know. You do an excellent job in making me realize I don't know anything." He laughed. "I always think I have some type of sense when it comes to life. I come in here and realize I know absolutely nothing."

"A wise person knows they really know nothing," the therapist said.

"Well, I guess that means I'm highly ignorant. I swear I know everything. Even when I'm wrong, I feel like I'll come up with the answer to be on the right side, and just continue to stay on the wrong side until then. What is wrong with me?"

"How do you feel?" he asked.

"What do you mean?"

"How do you feel when it comes to life in general? What's your views on relationships, love, morals, happiness, goals?" I took a deep breath.

"What if all my answers compromise the situation I'm in now?"

"Then I think you would answer a lot of questions without asking." I nodded my head. I think I know what he means, but am not sure, and don't want to ask him to elaborate. I treat him like a friend, a friend I have to pay for by the hour. It's sad that I must pay to feel a sense of being understood. It's amazing what the world has come to. I guess I'll leave now.

****

I've been searching for Christina for five days. I'm not sure if she's avoiding me because her dream was true, or if she's in one of her phases. She hasn't been home these past five days, or isn't answering the door, which would be very petty of her. Not hearing from her actually scares me. Someone that's having mental issues shouldn't be alone. I wonder does she know about my car accident.

Tiffany and Camille being friends really annoys me. I refuse to hang with them together, though Tiffany has begged me to. Maybe I should just end it all. I should just break ties with the both of them. Does not being in control of the situation really bother me that much? The answer is yes, hell yes. What types of conversations are they having? Camille knows so much about her, yet Tiffany knows so little. I'm giving myself a headache just from thinking on it.

They are having a "girl's day" today. What exactly is that? Tiffany isn't into gossip, so what exactly does she need to spend all day with a girl for? The thought is irritating me. Maybe I should hit up one of my guy friends. Now that I think about it, I don't really have any guy friends outside of my co-workers, only women. My mom was my only true friend and she's dead. I should have stayed with my therapist a little while longer. I really don't think about her until I need someone to talk to. By habit, I immediately pull out my phone and go to her name, which I haven't deleted yet. That just gave me an idea.

Being here makes me cringe. I thought I was ready for it, but now I see I'm wrong. I'm at my mom's grave. I came here to talk to her. I even had my speech in my head. Now that I'm here, I just want to cry. She really is dead. All I can do is look at the tombstone. I'm speechless, literally. All the words I want to say will not come out. I have to go.

I feel safe now that I'm back in my car. Graveyards aren't a good place to be. Now that I think about it, that's my first time being there. I skipped out on the funeral. Why didn't I think of that? There's no reason I should have been there. The situation is still too new. I haven't healed yet, though I want to. The sad thing is I don't know how to heal, if it's even possible. One thing I do know is I need a drink.

Tiffany just sent a text saying she's coming to my place after she leaves from hanging with Camille. A part of me wants to tell her not to come. Why would I do that? Not necessarily because of something she's done, more because of my ego. My ego is in a wounded spot. I've lost control over everything and don't know how to gain it back. My dad is calling me. Great, now he's going to be on my mind. I'm not answering this call.

We're lying in my room of adultery and it doesn't feel right. The air feels different. I washed them, but we're still on the same sheet and blanket. Why did no one ever tell me cheating would feel this way? It's glamorized everywhere I go. I'm not seeing the glamour in it.

"Baby, we need to talk," Tiffany softly said. Great, she can feel it in the air also. She knows I've done something in this room.

"No, we don't need to talk. I don't know what Camille has put into your head, but I do know whenever a woman says, "we need to talk," it's never a good thing." I smiled and looked at the ceiling. My smile is to cover my nervousness, only because I don't know what's about to come next. I can't say that Tiffany has changed. Maybe I'm imagining her changing because Camille's around.

"Camille hasn't told me anything besides you're a great worker, which I already knew. The friendship is growing and I love having her as a friend." So many thoughts are running through my head at the moment. I will not express them, I will keep them to myself. I feel like I'm leaving Tiffany in the dark about Camille's past situation. Would she still feel the same if she knew? Assuming that the situation is true.

"Baby, how do you feel about transgenders?" I asked.

"Well, that's a topic we've never talked about. I've never even felt that topic on our radar. What made you think about that? What are you doing while we're apart from each other? What type of porn are you watching?" I burst out laughing.

"I haven't watched porn in a very long time. Why watch porn when we can make our own tape?" My hand slid under the blanket, touching her vagina.

"I don't think you'd be up for the challenge. I'd imagine it being a totally different ballgame once the camera started recording." She grabbed two of my fingers and inserted them inside of her. She shivered and closed her eyes. I've immediately become erect, hard as a rock. Her phone rang.

"Don't answer it," I softly said.

"Baby, it's Camille." She answered the phone. Well, isn't this nice. I'm trying to get the mood right, trying to get the adultery energy out my room, and the person who is responsible for the adultery calls and ruins it all? How is this even possible? How can my luck be this bad? How? And now she's sitting on the phone talking to her, while I'm hard as a rock. Am I supposed to not be upset? She doesn't seem to be getting off the phone anytime soon. I guess I'll go to sleep.

"Marcus, you better not go to sleep." I've tuned her out. Am I being petty? Hell no I'm not. I can't even get the mood right without Camille being involved. They should cut me out the picture and become a couple. Maybe they are made for each other. Maybe that's what all of this really means. Maybe my hell was meant for them to form their heaven. I'm disgusted and I'm going to sleep. This has been a horrible night.

Chapter 6

"What are we doing?" Camille asked.

"What do you mean?" I asked, not trying to hide my annoyance.

"Isn't this crazy? We're cheating in plain sight. It's like we don't have to sneak around anymore, except for sexual purposes. This isn't how I imagined it."

"We're done," I bluntly stated.

"What?"

"We're done, I'm done. I can't do this anymore." I stood up from the restaurant table.

"You don't even love her." She motioned me to sit back down.

"I'm done with her too. I'm done with everything and everyone. I just want to be alone. I want to be alone from the world. I'm going to find a cave to permanently live in. You and Tiffany can become best friends for all I care. Everyone leave me alone." I stood up again.

"Is being in love with a former man bothering you?" she asked. I sat back down. "We've brought it up, but we've never talked about it from your point of view. I basically argued my point to keep you around. I need to know how you feel. I care about your feelings. I deeply care about you."

"I rather talk to my diary," I stated.

"Your diary doesn't give you feedback."

"You don't know what my diary gives me."

"Does it make you feel as good as I do?" she asked with a smile. The thoughts that are floating through my mind are probably thoughts I'd regret if I said them aloud. I'm angry on the inside. No, I'm angry and hurt, and I'm really not caring about anything at the moment.

"What if God didn't make a mistake with you? What if that was just your excuse to neglect that you may be emotionally and mentally damaged, to put it nicely." She took a sip of her water. How that question came out is totally different from how I had it worded in my head. I sometimes wish I wasn't a calm person. I wish I reacted to everything in a negative way.

"So, we're back to this topic, the topic you swore you were wrong about. Well, if I'm such a mentally and emotionally damaged person, and you've continued to engage with me on a social, mental, emotional, and sexual level, what does that make you, Marcus?" That's not the response I was expecting. How do I respond to that? Maybe she's right, even if I don't want to admit it to myself. "We've really arrived back to the topic of being emotionally damaged. Just say how you really feel. I'm a tough girl, I can handle it."

"You can think whatever you want, just know that I'm done. I'm starting over with life."

"Marcus, you've attempted to leave me multiple times. Some type of way you always find your way back to me. No, I'm not saying this in an arrogant way. I'm asking why continue to deny what is meant to be? What? You may be having conflicting feelings? That doesn't mean it isn't meant to be. You're trying to see the world for how you want it to be, not for what it already is."

"I've had enough of this conversation. Have a good life. You and Tiffany can become best friends and maybe start dating. Just leave me alone." I stood up and walked away. I'm not even paying for the meal, she can do it. Her words are stinging. It seems like each word pierced my heart. My heart may have a hole in it. I need someone to talk to but know not a soul will understand.

I keep a bottle of Hennessy under my passenger seat. This was a recent idea I thought would come in handy. Now I can sit here and drink in the parking lot of this restaurant. Now that I'm done with Camille, I need to figure out how to be done with Tiffany. I sometimes wish I was still in jail. The only thing to do in jail is think.

I reached my apartment. No, I'm not drunk, but I'm also not sober. I notice Tiffany's car and now remember she's spending the next few days with me. She doesn't know that we're done as a couple, and since I haven't figured it out yet, I'm not going inside until I do, even if that means I must sleep in my car.

I opened my eyes. I hear a knock on the window. I'm willing to bet a million dollars it's Tiffany, without even looking. I turned on my car. Yes, I'm avoiding glancing to my left. I don't want to see Tiffany's expression. I'm going to decline when she calls me asking what's wrong. I don't even know what's exactly wrong, I just know that I'm losing my sense of reasoning for living. I really miss my mom.

I pulled up to my therapist's home. No, I don't have an appointment, and yes, I know it's going to disappoint him with me just coming over, especially to his home and not his practice. Oh well, get over it. I'll still pay him for the session, which is all that should matter. I reached his door and knocked.

"Well, this is a surprise," he said as he opened the door. I walked past him. Wow, his living room looks very similar to the room of his practice. He has a couch very similar to the one I like to lay on. It may actually be the same, just a different color.

"What if I told you I was a homosexual?" I asked to the therapist. I stretched out on the couch. It feels better than the other one. I may have to make this couch my new home. He can take all my money. This is my new place of comfort. The energy here feels different than it does outside. This is the type of energy I wish was present at my place.

"Well, that would be a game changer concerning our conversations."

"What if I told you I was confused?"

"I would ask you to elaborate." My mind and heart says to tell my problems to this man. I've written inside my diary that I wouldn't, but I'm tired of holding it in. I don't have all the answers, though I try to tell myself I do. I need clarity.

"Is it possible to turn feelings off?" I asked.

"Anything is possible, technically speaking." I sighed.

"Here are my thoughts. I feel like we can't control our feelings, but can control acting on them. But what if it literally kills you when you don't act on the feeling? Though the results of acting on the feeling is bad for you, not physically, but more on an emotional level, because where you are getting the results from is a complicated piece of energy. Am I making sense?"

"Are you done?" he asked.

"Everything and everyone is energy. So, my energy and another person's energy is connecting to create a powerful energy that seems good, but may be wrong because one of our energies are conflicting. Maybe both of our energies are conflicting, complicated energies. Is it possible for two souls of very conflicting energies to create something positive? Or is it all an illusion? Are the souls telling themselves the energy is positive, when they both are truly in denial?"

"You are telling me everything without telling me anything at all, if that makes sense." I want to turn and look him in the eyes, but will continue to look at the ceiling.

"I want you to read between the lines. You're the psychiatrist, therapist, and psychologist. You're extremely smart. Yes, I did my research before coming to you. Do I sound like I'm crazy to you?"

"Crazy is such a vague word. I don't think anyone is really crazy. I think we all process our thoughts differently, which may cause some of us to act on things differently. There's a lot of things that could go into making a person 'crazy,' or any other vague word."

"So, you're saying that I process my thoughts in a bad way?"

"I'm sure we all process our thoughts in a bad way to someone. No one is perfect." I really wish he would tell me what I want to hear. "You know, since you've came here you haven't truly stated a situation or problem you're going through. You tend to ask questions revolving around the actual question, if that makes sense." I took a deep breath.

"Sometimes questions sound better in your mind. There's a fear of actually putting the question into the universe. The self-torture is real. The questions linger in my mind daily. Then there's that fear of you being human. What if you don't have the answers to my questions? That's quite possible, you can't know everything. I don't want those questions left in the universe unanswered. What can I say? You're the paid friend I just enjoy talking to."

"So, you're saying you only talk to me because you pay me?" I nodded my head.

"Have you not seen the outside world? Keeping a secret no longer exists. I'm not even sure people are aware of how much they talk, and the things they are talking about. A lot of things I hear people say I truly believe were meant for a private conversation. With you, it's against the law to expose our conversations, unless I'm doing something violent to an individual. People like you don't exist in the real world."

"I'm the only person you feel you can open up to?"

"I can't even trust my significant other with my thoughts anymore, and this is supposed to be the girl I'm marrying. It's amazing how my life has turned upside down." There's a knock on his door. Has someone randomly come over needing a session?

"That's my wife. She has groceries in her hands and can't get to her keys to open the door. Call my office and set up an appointment so we can continue this conversation." I nodded my head and stood up.

"Will she have a problem with me randomly showing up here? Does she need help with the groceries? I had no clue you were married." I looked down at his hand. His marriage ring is there, and probably has always been there. I've just had horrible attention to detail lately.

"My wife will be fine. You're not the first person to do this. She knows these types of actions come with the job. It's one of the many things she had to accept when she decided to marry me." I nodded my head and walked towards the front door. I wish Tiffany could accept the many things that comes with marrying me.

****

"What makes you think I'm the one?" I asked Camille. It's only been a week since I told her we were done.

"I made dinner. Are you hungry?" I really can't go longer than a week without seeing her. What is wrong with me?

"Are you going to answer my question? And no, I'm not hungry." She sat down by me. My last conversation with Tiffany has me in a weird spot. I'm drowning in guilt and confusion. I never knew I meant so much to her, or maybe she just doesn't mean that much to me. This is supposed to be the woman I'm marrying.

"Why wouldn't you be the one?" she asked.

"Camille, that's not what I asked." I don't know why, but I'm highly annoyed. Tiffany's words won't leave my head. We had a conversation since Camille ruined our sexual moment that is unforgettable. The conversation did nothing but accelerate my drown into confusion. She also accepted my apology for driving off on her. I may be taking her for granted.

"How do you expect me to explain the unexplainable? You really expect me to explain my feelings?" This sounds similar to what I said to my therapist. "Well, I can't describe them. I do know you make me feel good, everything about you. Your flaws make me feel good, which is crazy. You put my mind at ease. I've never believed in anything everlasting until I met you. I've only believed in anything only lasting ninety days. You have me believing in years."

"What if your belief is wrong?"

"What if my belief is right?" she asked back. I'm not sure what I expected to get out of this conversation. Maybe I'm hoping for some type of sign, a sign that Tiffany is the one and this is all a mistake. Maybe my feelings are wrong. I thought I had a slight understanding for the heart, but am now realizing I don't know anything when it comes to feelings. Why would the heart allow me to feel for someone that isn't right? "Marcus, I love you."

"I love you too."

"Are you sure?"

"I'm not sure of anything," I truthfully replied. I need clear clarification on if being with Camille would make me a homosexual, though I'm still hoping for the text saying this is all a joke. I have nothing against homosexuality, but never imagined me being one. They say most homosexuals are born that way, which may or may not be true. I can't relate to that. I love women with a passion. But, my dad is a homosexual. Was he born that way and tried to fight it? Is it in my DNA?

"Marcus, what are you thinking about? You have a habit of getting quiet, like you've gone into deep thought."

"You don't want to know my thoughts, trust me. I don't even want to know my thoughts, and I'm the one that's thinking them. My head is going to explode one day." I don't think I'd be considered a homosexual. I fell for a woman on the outside. I honestly wish she never told me. I was better off not knowing. Why would she damage my mind with these thoughts? I'm not sure if I could forgive her if this is a joke. It's really affecting me on all levels.

"If you're not the one, how do you always find your way back to me?" she asked. "You've walked away about three times. Some type of way you find your soul back to mine. We'd be lying to ourselves if we didn't admit that we have a connection."

"What kind of connection do we have?"

"Marcus, you tell me. Express your heart to me." I sighed. Sometimes I wish I didn't have a heart. Having a heart is probably why I'm in this predicament. Why can't I be heartless? Why must I drown in guilt and confusion? I just….. I don't know what I want. "Out of curiosity, who do you love more? Tiffany or me?" Why ask me such a difficult question? She's not helping anything.

"I'm not sure." I got up and walked out of her apartment. I'm tired of being confused. This is mentally exhausting. I miss my mom. Problems were much easier to solve when she was alive. I now feel alone, trying to figure everything out. I feel homeless on the inside. I feel like I have no friends, no family, no associates, nothing. I feel like I'm just living, going through life with a blindfold over my eyes. I have no direction and I'm accepting it. I'm giving up on life.

I love driving with no destination. Yes, I'm just wasting gas, but driving around is a stress reliever. I've sometimes driven so long that I've ended up in another state. I want to leave Florida. I want to leave the United States. If it was up to me I'd move to Argentina and start over. Why Argentina? I don't know, it's the last place I think someone would search for me. Too bad Tiffany wouldn't do it. Why am I not just thinking about me?

I need to hurry up and make a decision. Who is it going to be, Tiffany or Camille? I've tried weighing the pros and cons, and the answer I've come up with is I should be with neither. I should just be by myself and live in my mind. I just want to sit in a room and live with my sins until I accept them, if I ever accept them. That sounds like self-torture, which is probably what I need. It's hard to forgive myself when I'm still indulging in the same sins.

I really proposed to Tiffany. What am I doing? Well, it's too late to take that back. We've already found a date for the wedding. I still can't believe she forgave me for driving off on her. I wonder will the wedding be the happiest or worst day of my life. It probably will be both. My phone is ringing. If this wasn't Christina I'm sure I wouldn't answer it. I've been searching for her, now she mysteriously pops up. "Christina," I answered, "Where in the world have you been? I've been searching everywhere for you."

"I was back in the psych ward, spending time with all my friends. I accidently had a beer, and let's just say the effects weren't good. I was hanging with a friend and she says I caused a scene. The psych ward is such a peaceful place for me. A lot of people there are screaming at the top of their lungs all through the night, and I'm sitting in my padded room feeling comfortable."

"Shit."

"Marcus, when did you get such a foul mouth?"

"I really didn't know what else to say. Are you still there? Well, you can't be. You're calling me from your phone."

"No, I'm still here. I just asked for my phone for a minute. I'm displaying my normal tendencies. I don't think I want to leave here. I feel completely safe here." There's so many things I want to say, but I will refrain.

"Christina, come stay with me. You can have my room. I'll get the couch."

"Absolutely not! I wouldn't dare live with you. You're a cheater!" I burst out laughing.

"Christina, that's kind of harsh, don't you think?" I just remembered that this is our first time talking since she showed up to my apartment. I would prefer this conversation face to face. "Whoever said I was actually cheating? I never admitted to anything. You're accusing me with no actual proof."

"Marcus, you're going to make me leave this psych ward just to come fuck you up. I'll fuck you up and happily come back to this psych ward."

"And you say I have a foul mouth."

"Your expression told the story. I know what you're about to say. You're going to say your expression didn't confirm anything. Your expression was meant to show shock that my dream potentially had some truth to it." It's scary that she knows me so well. I don't think Tiffany knows me as well as Christina. "Am I wrong? Tell me I'm wrong? I'll leave this psych ward right now."

"Well, you're wrong," I happily said. The call ended. Well, that phone call went great. Maybe I should let this drive take me to another state. If Christina really does see me, she may.... I don't know what she's going to do. I wonder about her thought process a lot. Her thinking patterns are different from most people. Is that what drugs do to you? I've thought about trying drugs, but I know I have an addictive personality, and tend to get addicted to things quickly. That's also a big reason I'm scared to try coffee.

Somehow, I've ended up in Georgia, which means I've been driving for hours. Part of me says to keep driving, keep driving until you get to Seattle. I don't know what's in Seattle, I just know it's completely on the other side of the country, and I'll be far away from my problems. With my luck, my problems will just follow me. I'm going to keep driving.

It's amazing to think my life was perfect just a few months ago. I want to blame someone else but can only blame myself. How is it possible to ruin a great situation? While I'm worrying about Christina's thought process, I need to be worried about mine. I need to talk to my therapist. I really want to be transparent with him. At this point, I'd be transparent with anyone if I felt they'd truly understand me.

****

"Marcus, where have you been?" Tiffany asked. I got out the car and attempted to hug her. She moved to avoid my embrace. "You can't just go missing for three days." I just realized that my life has turned into one cycle of the same events. The interesting part is that the cycle hasn't turned into happiness.

"I think I'm having a mid-life crisis," I truly admitted. I really contemplated not coming back. I'd basically said fuck everything. The problem with that mindset is when you have no plan, it's actually hard to execute on that thought. I ended up in Arkansas and it made me realize that I was making a huge mistake. My escape from life needs to be planned.

"Marcus, how are you having a mid-life crisis?" You can hear the concern in her voice. How do you explain to someone you care about that you're not sure if you're in love with them anymore? I don't even love myself anymore. How can I walk around with all these conflicting emotions and still have two people wanting love from me? Maybe we're all crazy.

"I miss my mom." I feel myself wanting to cry. She hugged me and kissed me on my cheek. I wonder what Mom's opinion would be on how I'm living right now. She's probably rolling in her grave. I'm sure she couldn't imagine me living this way because I couldn't imagine it. I wonder if there's a right way to deal with death. There could be a book on it, which has made me realize that I've been slacking on my book reading.

"I know you do," Tiffany started, "And know you have to deal with it every day. I've admitted that I don't know how to nurture you in this process, and I'm failing as a friend and a fiancé. I can't tell you I understand, or I feel your pain. I'm sad, but I know it doesn't compare to your sadness. I'm having a hard time accepting that I can't help you. I also use that as a reason to not get extremely mad when you get distant. I just get mad because I miss you."

"You have a unique way of making me feel guilty," I said with a smile. We walked inside her apartment. Why did I come here instead of going directly to my place? Maybe the universe attracted me here to be in these moments. This is what love is supposed to feel like. Her way of making me feel guilty puts a warmth in my heart that I haven't felt in a long time.

"Baby, this might not be the right time to ask, but when is the last time we've had sex?" Am I supposed to know the answer to this question? I can't even give an estimate on that timeframe. I really suck as a boyfriend.

"The last time doesn't matter when we can do it now." I kissed her on the lips. How do I go from being in a mid-life crisis to becoming horny? I have no clue, and I guess it shouldn't matter. I need to get back to what I'm good at, and that's pleasing Tiffany. It's hard now that I feel like I have to also please everyone else. So much for having my priorities in order.

Dear Diary,

Demons and angels, I'm not sure if I know the difference anymore. I hear that you're supposed to fight your demons. How do you defeat something you enjoy playing with? Does that mean I'm in love with misery? I swear, I'm starting to hate the process of writing my thoughts down. When I read them, I really think to myself that I'm crazy. But when I keep them inside my head, I also think I'm going crazy. What is wrong with me? Next subject, I've really been thinking about relapsing. I rather walk around numb. Being in reality, being in the moment is for idiots. My mind is never quiet. All I hear is voices in my head 24/7. That just leads to me having these fucked up, scary dreams. I don't know which is worse, being up or being sleep. I'm being tortured either way. I never had these problems when I was doing drugs. I can't even use sex for an escape. I'm NEVER horny, literally. I watch tons of porn and nothing happens. Shit, why can't I be normal? It makes me want to scream! I tried masturbating last week, and it's like nothing happened. I couldn't even get wet. Why me? The doctors say it's because of my over usage of drugs, then I stopped cold turkey so it's severely damaged my hormones. They have a pill that can help repair my hormones, but it's 800 dollars! Who can afford that? Why not spend time with my demons? What if my demons and angels are the same? Is that possible? I'm just trying to find happiness. Too bad the journey to happiness didn't come with directions.

Christina

"Where are your parents?" I asked. "How do they feel about everything?"

"They want to be in my life, but I won't allow them. They're probably blaming themselves for me being damaged. They're probably telling themselves they could have loved me more. I don't blame them, I blame me. It's all my fault."

"Your parents don't love you?" I've always liked Christina's parents. They were insane enough to let me stay the night during the weekdays, like they were just positive Christina and I wasn't having sex. We never did, and if we did I don't remember it. I'll blame the liquor for that. I'm just realizing that Christina is cute. I guess when you've actually grown up with a person since being children it never crosses your mind. I would feel some type of way if we would have slept together in the past. She's a totally different person.

"I mean, I think they love me. You used to be around them. Did they seem like they loved me?" I nodded my head. "How do you know? You were probably drunk while being around my parents." I burst out laughing. I really don't remember much of anything. I remember scenes in life. What's sad is that all the scenes I remember aren't important scenes. I don't even remember losing my virginity, just the person. She asked me a few days later why hadn't I mentioned us having sex. Of course I didn't have an answer.

"You're right, I really don't remember much. Don't tell anyone. You and my mom are the only people that know."

"How do you deal with it?" Christina asked.

"How do I deal with what?"

"How do you deal with your mom being in a coma? How do you deal with knowing you have no control over the situation? There's nothing you can say or do that will make her wake up. I've had these thoughts myself and it truly makes me go insane. My voices get to telling me answers I don't want to hear. I start screaming that she will wake up. Then I start crying because I'm not sure if I'm right or not." I feel so guilty for not telling Christina my mom is dead. Now isn't the right time.

"I don't think I deal with it at all. I just go through the motions. Thinking about her saddens me, so I try not to think about her. I really can't explain it. I'm almost numb to it. I don't want to give any feelings to it. Any feelings to it won't change the fact she's in a coma. All I can do is hope she wakes up soon and continue to live until she does."

"That's such a narcissistic answer," she said. She shook her head.

"Everything I say is considered narcissistic to you," I shot back.

"You're so into yourself. You're the only person I know who's afraid of people, afraid to get help. You walk around like you just know you're going to figure everything out on your own, like God doesn't exist. You do know God put other people on this earth, right? That means we are connected. We are supposed to help each other!"

"How do we help each other? The person you're asking for help has their own set of problems that they can't even solve. Why be vulnerable with a person when they're only going to think about themselves first? Am I the only person with a functioning brain in the universe?" I should mention that I'm going to a therapist. He's not really helping me, he's just an ear to hear my thoughts.

"How are you going to say that when you have a significant other in your life? How is that even possible? Can a narcissist really have a significant other? Now that I think about it, you're cheating on her. It all makes sense now."

"I'm not cheating on Tiffany."

"You're just a fucked up individual, Marcus. You're just damaged and don't care about being repaired. I just realized it. No, I'm not judging you."

"Do you really have the credibility to call me a damaged person, like seriously?"

"The difference between you and I is that I'm not in denial about my problems. I know I'm insane in the head. I know I'm not normal. I tell myself I'm perfectly fine with the attempt of falling asleep at night. My dream then reminds me that I lied myself to sleep. So, when I wake up I then just relive the thoughts. I know I need help. I even write my thoughts down AND let you read them. You think I enjoy letting you know I'm not the same girl?"

"What's the point in this conversation?" I asked.

"You know what? Marcus, just leave. Talking to you is like talking to a brick wall. I don't know what you're emotionally going through, but I wish you the best. I only can wish because I know you're going to push away any help that comes your way. You figure your life out and I'll try to do the same." I nodded my head. "Marcus, where is the emotion?"

"We are only as dark and sick as our secrets," I replied.

"What does that even mean?" I opened the door and left. The nerve of her. Where's the emotions? I'm full of emotions! Just because I have an unorthodox way of showing them doesn't mean they don't exist. Openly displaying my emotions will be me giving in to defeat. I'm not ready to give up on life again, so I'll just hold it all in. I like the internal battle. I think we were put here in this world to see how much pain we can endure before going insane. Only the strong survive.

Chapter 7

"Marcus, are you cheating on me?" Fear has leaped into my heart. I know I must stay calm. Any loud reaction will be an admission of guilt. I wish we were in a public setting just in case this conversation goes wrong. I can't run, even if I wanted to while being at her place.

"Tiffany, why would you think that? Yes, I'm shocked that you're asking me this question. Where did the question come from?"

"I've just noticed a few things that's been different about you lately." I guess this is the beginning of the end. Maybe this is my chance to be free like I've claimed I've wanted since catching feelings for Camille. Or I can just admit to myself that I don't know what I want, but that would make me just like everyone else in the world. My first thought is Camille has told her, but I don't think Camille is that messy of a person.

"Please, elaborate."

"Are you sleeping with someone else when we're having sex?"

"What!" I shouted.

"Did you not hear my question? When we are having sex together, are you having sex with someone else mentally? Are you visualizing someone else during our sex?"

"What in the hell would make you think of a question like that?" This conversation has gone somewhere I wasn't expecting. Scared isn't a strong enough word to describe how Tiffany has me feeling at the moment. The thoughts that go through people's minds.

"The passion."

"The passion?" I asked. "What does that even mean?"

"The passion of the sex is more passionate than how you feel about me." Are these the types of thoughts that go through people's minds? Really?

"How do you know how high or low my passion levels are towards you?"

"Marcus, we've been together for years, and I've mentioned before that you lack a layer of passion. Recently that layer of passion has been present."

"So, because you've noticed an unexpected layer of passion, that means I'm cheating on you? That makes absolutely no sense at all."

"Where does the passion come from?" I don't have an answer. I'm actually stuck right now. How do I get myself out of this situation? Usually an answer comes to me quickly, even if it's a stupid answer. Right now, nothing is coming. I'm shaking on the inside. I'm not sure if it's because of the actual question or because I feel like I've been caught.

"I don't know," I started, "I didn't notice the passion I was giving off. Maybe the fact we're getting married has played a role. Maybe me realizing you're all I have left is playing a role."

"You haven't spoken to me about your dad and your childhood neglect. All you've ever mentioned is that he left you as a kid. That could really be affecting you right now."

"Fuck him. That's my answer to any question you may want to ask about him. I haven't discussed him because it leaves nothing but anger in my heart. I wish he was dead instead of my mom. I'll never forgive him for leaving me. The combination of him leaving me and my mom now being dead has shattered my world. The best thing for me to do is to accept it and move on."

"It's going to be alright, Marcus." She walked towards me and hugged me. I told the truth for a change and it rescued me from a bad situation.

Tiffany has her doubts, and I claim I want to leave, but am trying to fight her doubts away. What type of sense does that make? I miss when everything was normal. I miss just having one focus, one world. When Tiffany was my world nothing else mattered. My life had more structure and it was genuine. Love one person, go to work, and let everything else fall into place.

Now, I love an alleged transgender, my mom is dead, and my dad has another son he loves more than the son he left behind. My life is chaos now. I'm not going to blame this situation, but it seems like life changed for the worse once Camille came into the picture. It seems like a domino effect of horrible events happened. Does that mean she represents bad luck? Maybe I'm thinking too much.

I need to talk to my mom. She always seemed to have all the answers. Mom, how do you leave me here to learn for myself when you've always had my back? Google doesn't have the answers you had. Maybe you don't have all the answers. Maybe I just miss the conversations. I don't even know the type of answers Mom would give me today. I was headed down this path when she was alive and didn't come to her. I probably wouldn't come to her today. The people and things we take for granted is amazing when I think about it. We actually take time for granted. We spend time with people like we know we're going to see the person tomorrow. Maybe it's just me.

I'm at work physically, but somewhere else mentally. I just realized something. I live in my head a lot. I think I live more in my head than in reality, almost like a virtual world. I'm not sure if it's always been this way, or if this is something new. My thoughts haven't been the best lately, so honestly, I'm not sure which life is better. My thoughts are dark, my reality is dark. Why am I living again?

"Tiffany is here," a female co-worker whispered in my ear. I'm stuck in my chair. Shit, Tiffany is here. She's going to ask to come in. When she comes in she will see that my supervisor is a man and there's no Camille as a supervisor. There's no Camille as a co-worker. Why couldn't she call me? She usually calls when she's on her way and I'd meet her outside. This was before Camille came into the picture.

"Hey love," I said with a smile. My smile is clearly to hide the fear and fast heartbeat. "What are you doing here? I didn't know you were off today?"

"Well, I wanted to have lunch with my fiancé, so I decided to take the day off. I was hoping Camille could come down and have lunch with us." I think my heart just stopped. "That reminds me, I've never seen the inside of your job before. You've been working here since I met you, and you've been inside of my job before. Do you mind if I go in and check it out? I'd like to see how your job operates." Any answer outside of the obvious answer would cause suspicion.

"Camille is actually conducting a team meeting for the next forty-five minutes that I'm supposed to be attending. I wish you would have called before coming. I would have told you to wait for an hour. But hey, screw that meeting, I will sit down and have lunch with you. If I get fired, you can always take care of me because technically it will be your fault." She burst out laughing.

"I don't think you would let me take care of you, even if you really needed it." I nodded my head. It would feel weird letting her take care of me. I would look for another way to make money. My mom had a six-figure life insurance policy. I haven't mentioned it to Tiffany yet. That's my insurance policy for a worst-case scenario.

Lunch was delicious. It was just what I needed. I now want to take a nap. Tiffany's phone is ringing. "Baby, it's Camille." My heart just stopped. "Does that mean the meeting is over and I can go inside now?"

"Don't answer it," I quickly responded. Let me slow down. "She's probably calling you to ask if I'm with you. If I bring you in she will then know I skipped the meeting to be with you. I know we're all friends, that doesn't mean she wouldn't be forced to make an example out of me." She nodded her head in agreement.

"Well, I'm going to let you get back to work. I will see you tonight." She got up and walked away. I now can breathe a sigh of relief. That was too close. If I was an angry person I'd probably curse Camille out the next time I talked to her. Luckily, I'm not an angry person. Now I have to go back in here and explain to my supervisor why I took an early lunch break.

"Marcus, I need a favor?" This scares me. I can't remember the last time Christina asked me for a favor, if ever.

"What is it?"

"Have sex with me." My eyes just widened.

"What? I think I heard you wrong."

"Have sex with me," she restated.

"Hell no!" I replied.

"Why not?" she asked. Is she losing her mind? Or am I not comprehending her request?

"Christina, why in the hell would I do that?"

"What? You don't find me attractive? Am I ugly? You know I have an internal problem. What? You're too good to help a friend out? You like seeing me suffer?" She pulled her sweatpants and panties down.

"Christina! What in the hell are you doing?" I looked away. What is going on right now? Am I having a nightmare? This can't be real. She laid on her bed. I can see her out my side view.

"Come lick me down there."

"Christina, I'm not looking over there."

"Marcus, stop being a pussy. Help your best friend out! I don't ask you for much!"

"I thought you said you can't get horny."

"I'm not horny now. That's the problem! If you stop being a pussy and look over here, you'd see that I'm not even wet. Just lick it a few times. I want to see what happens."

"Christina, I'm not licking your vagina. You're a cute girl. I'm sure there's plenty of men that will do it." She sucked her teeth.

"It's called a pussy! Who says vagina? And I need you to lick it. You're the only person that understands me. Do you know how awkward it will be if someone else licks me and nothing happens? Stop thinking about yourself for a second and look over here!"

"Christina, I'm not looking in your direction. Please put your panties and sweatpants back on." This has to be one of the most awkward moments ever. I'm really at a loss for words. I refuse to look in her direction. I'm not even curious to see her body parts. I feel a headache coming.

"Marcus, you're acting like I'm asking you to stick your dick in. I'm only asking for a few licks. You're already cheating on Tiffany. A few licks won't hurt anyone! This isn't for sexual pleasure. It's for psychological reasons!"

"I'm not cheating on Tiffany, and there will be no tongue to vagina contact. Now, put your sweatpants back on, please."

"Pussy," she mumbled. I hear her moving. I'm assuming she's getting back dressed. At least that's what I'm hoping. I need a drink; I want to quickly forget about this day, this moment, this life. I can't even imagine having sex with Christina. Some things just don't seem right. "Ok, pussy, my sweatpants are back on." I turned around.

"That's not my name. Anyways, I'll give you the 800 dollars for the hormones pill if you really feel like you need it. No, I just don't have 800 dollars to happily give, but if you really feel like you're suffering down there, I'll give it to you." She shook her head.

"So, you rather give me 800 dollars that you really don't have for hormone pills, when you can lick me for free? Marcus, do you hear how stupid you sound? Am I the only person thinking right now?

"I'm not licking your vagina."

"Stop calling it a vagina!" I gave her a thumbs-down. I really want to tell Tiffany about this, just for her feedback. I just remembered she hasn't met Christina yet. I've talked about Christina a few times but refused to mention the part about Christina being different. Christina can stay sane for short periods of time. I've noticed her tendencies when she starts battling the voices she's hearing in her head. I have to keep that in mind for both of our benefits. "I just want to let you know you're selfish."

"Thank you for the compliment," I said with a smile. "So, are you going to take the money or continue to complain?" She sucked her teeth.

"You make me sound like some type of prostitute." I burst out laughing. "If those are my only choices, I rather continue to complain. I'm so upset with you. So, when are you going to let me meet your girlfriend?"

"First, you ask me to lick your vagina, now you want to meet my girlfriend?" I burst out laughing. "You have a funny way of doing things." Christina looks like she wants to punch me in the face right now. "You will meet her when the time is right."

"The right time is right now. Call her, tell her you have a best friend that wants to meet her." I shook my head in disagreement. "What's wrong with my idea?"

"I have to prepare that situation correctly." Christina threw her hands up.

"Here you go, always trying to be in control of everything. Sometimes you have to let things naturally flow." I pulled out my phone. "What are you doing?"

"Telling Tiffany to meet us at the park where we rekindled this friendship." She smiled and got off the bed. I have a feeling I'm making a huge mistake. Hopefully I'm wrong, but in these types of situations I'm never wrong. I'm ignoring my gut feeling, trying not to be a narcissist.

This is a silent car ride. I'm just thinking of everything that could go wrong. For every possibility, I need to have a lie prepared. It's sad that I'm premeditating lies, but it's better to be safe than sorry. Christina is unpredictable; I never know what she's going to say.

We pulled up to the park. Tiffany is already standing outside of her car. I now wish I never met back up with Christina at this exact park. It all seems like one big mistake. Why am I being so negative? Maybe this will go good. I actually don't know what a good outcome will consist of. We got out the car. Tiffany has a glow to her today.

"Tiffany, this is my best friend, Christina. Christina, this is my fiancé, Tiffany." They shook hands. My heart is beating fast. Maybe I just need to breathe. I read in a book that most of the terrible things we think will happen rarely does, so we're really just torturing ourselves.

"Marcus, you didn't tell me you were engaged. You've been mentioning her since I've been back around and forgot to mention that part." Shit, how do I forget to mention that? It was an honest mistake.

"I've heard a lot about you," Tiffany started, "I'm happy to finally put a face to the great personality." Christina nodded and smiled. I know that smile and the thoughts behind it. She's trying to put the pieces together. She's thinking I didn't mention I was engaged, so that confirms her theory that I'm cheating on Tiffany. She's also wondering what part of her personality have I described to Tiffany. I would never tell anyone about her other side. I'm big on loyalty. Any conversations I have with an individual is kept between us two.

"So, when are the two of you moving in together, since you are engaged?" she asked with a smile. This is her way of telling me she's mad at me. She knows I'm hiding my alcoholism. She knows I'm an emotional wreck. She knows I'm not ready for marriage.

"That's actually a great question." Tiffany's glare turned to me. "Marcus, when are we moving in together?" I've been lying to her since I met Camille. Why does lying now feel much worse? "I remember you bringing it up, but that was the last time you mentioned it. I'm starting to feel like you purposely forgot."

"Well, maybe we should start searching for a place tomorrow," I said with a smile. I mean, what else am I supposed to say? I just pressed the accelerator to the destruction of my life. Thanks Christina. Thanks a lot.

****

"Is it scary that I may love you more than I love myself?" Camille asked. She always asks me these thought provoking questions when we're in the car. I guess it's harder for me to attempt to run away. I should just get out and leave the car here.

"I guess I should ask why do you think you love me more than you love yourself."

"You accept me, right?" She's asking me a question I'm still trying to avoid asking myself. I've planned on living and letting the answer reveal itself. Why must so many questions be asked? Why can't we just live life? Tiffany always says that in the future the only way to make money will be by being able to ask great questions. Great, now I'm thinking about Tiffany.

"I love you, doesn't that tell you everything?"

"Not really. You love me, but what do you love about me? You may just love my sex. You may just love my company when you don't want to be around Tiffany. You may just love the thought of loving me, which means you really don't love me at all. So, Marcus, why do you love me?"

"How did we get on the topic of love?" I have a headache, maybe because she's making me think too much. My brain is on thought overload. When did my life become so complicated? I want things to go back to normal, whatever normal consists of.

"Are you going to answer the question?" she asked in an annoyed tone.

"What was the question?" She squinted her eyes at me. "What? You said a lot. My brain can only process so much information at one time." She opened the door and got out. I'm not sure what that means but I'm thankful for her choice. I need time to think clearly. One thing her and Tiffany have in common is their ability to suffocate the air with their presence. They both have a strong energy. It's an energy I thought I loved, but now feel I need to get away from. How did I become so confused about life? A few months ago, I truly felt like I had everything figured out. It's funny how things have changed.

"Mom, if you're looking down on me from heaven, please tell God to give me some type of guidance. Give me some type of sign, redirect my path, remove all the unnecessary people out of my life." I don't pray much, but it felt good to say that out loud. Hopefully my mom hears me.

"Misha, what do you know about Camille?" I have a beer in my hand but want to stay focused on this conversation. Meeting at a bar was a good idea. I have to stay calm in here. I can't have an outburst around these people. The conversation I just had with Camille reminded me this is Misha's fault. I texted her asking her to meet me here.

"She's my best friend. I know everything about her. Do you like her? Are the two of you talking? I won't tell Tiffany if you like her, though I really love Tiffany. She has a beautiful soul." I have to make sure I word my question properly.

"Let's say I did like Camille. How would you feel about that?" She took a sip from her soda. I just realized Misha doesn't have any liquor in her cup. Yes, this is very unusual. Maybe she doesn't want to be intoxicated while driving.

"That would be an interesting choice to have feelings for."

"What does that even mean?" I feel myself getting annoyed. I'm not sure if she knows that Camille and I have this situation going on. Wow, I just realized Camille and I aren't in a relationship. How did these feelings get involved?

"Do the two of you communicate as friends?"

"Misha, Camille is supposedly a transgender," I calmly stated. Misha gasped and put her hand over her mouth.

"Wow, she told you?"

"Did she tell me? Why in the hell didn't you tell me? I thought we were family. What type of shit is that to do to your cousin?"

"Well, first of all, I had no plans of you talking to her. I didn't plan on bringing her to you at the party. It's almost like fate happened. My husband was calling from Iraq, so I quickly walked away to answer the phone. Second, technically, you didn't have to talk to her."

"The moment was awkward, I had to say something. What was I supposed to do? Stand there in silence and wait for you to come back?"

"Pretty much," she bluntly replied.

"You didn't come back!" Faces shifted in our direction. I thought being at the bar would keep my temper calm. I now see that I'm wrong. I don't have anger problems, but do have an uncontrollable outburst at times. My outburst has probably exposed that I have feelings for Camille. Shit, I have to reverse this. I can't let the secret out yet.

"Marcus, calm down."

"I apologize for the outburst. As you can see, the beer is having an effect on me. I don't have any type of feelings for Camille, but I do think she's cool, and will admit that I do enjoy our conversations. How is she a man?"

"She is not a man. She's obviously a woman. She has a pussy. I've seen it before." I feel a headache coming. Am I looking at this wrong? I swear my head is going to explode from thinking so much. "There's nothing wrong with liking a transgender."

"I never said I liked her," I shot back. My beer has lost its taste for some reason. I need tequila now.

"Well, you like the conversations, so you must like something about her. She didn't tell me you two were talking. Maybe she likes you. She doesn't keep secrets from me. What are you going to do about Tiffany?

"What do you mean? You ask that question like I have feelings for Camille and plan on leaving Tiffany. I'll never leave Tiffany. I just feel weird talking to Camille now that she's told me her secret. My reasoning could be wrong. You shouldn't have brought her around me." Misha smiled and shook her head. "I still don't believe it's true."

"What will happen if you seriously start liking her?" Misha asked with excitement.

"I won't start liking her."

"You never know. We as people can't control our feelings, even when we call ourselves trying. And if it makes you feel better, I didn't know her before the sex change. You never know, she could be lying. It could be for attention though I doubt it."

"Referring to your statement about feelings, that may be true, but we can control acting on them." It just clicked in my mind. My last statement just put everything in perspective. This is all my fault. It doesn't matter if she's lying or not, it's still all on me.

Chapter 8

Dear Diary,

You ever lie to yourself so much that you forget what the truth is? My life is falling apart. Tiffany and I now live together. What made us think this would be a good idea? We both like distance, why would we try to change that? I now feel cluttered. Everything doesn't feel special like it used to. There used to be a feeling of missing her. Not seeing her for a few days seemed to cause an emptiness, so when I finally did see her I was happy because I felt fulfilled. That emptiness is gone. I don't like this new normal. It's harder to have a drink and it's killing me. I'm lucky if I'm able to drink once a week now. I've now come to the realization that I'm beyond an alcoholic. You never know how much you need something until you're forced to go without it. I used to say that Tiffany makes me not want to drink. I think that's because the moments we shared felt more special. Now it feels like the moments are becoming more of a routine. I don't feel like she's changed. She's the same Tiffany she's always been. It's more of me being out of my comfort zone. I've committed to getting married and won't back out. I didn't want to get married before this decision to move in together. I definitely don't want to get married now. I feel more like a slave. I want to go back to how it used to be, but don't want to confront Tiffany. I don't want her to think she's the reason behind my mental and emotional states of unhappiness. Tiffany isn't the reason for any of my unhappiness. Tiffany isn't the reason for anything wrong in my life, but someone has to take the blame. I have strong urges for Camille, and I'm upset that I can't see her the way I want. No, I have to fight the urges. Maybe that's why this was a good idea. How did my life get to this point? I'm nowhere close to being mentally or emotionally stable. I never dreamed of being in love with two people. I've always aimed to be what I thought my dad should be, which is a good husband and father. I've always wanted to treat Tiffany how I felt my mom should be treated. Maybe I was trying the impossible. It can't be impossible. For years, I was on the right track. Where did I go wrong? The easy thing to do would be to let go of Camille. She's the cancer in my relationship. She's come to wreck everything. She's the true source of my unhappiness. My phone is ringing. Guess who it is?

Marcus

"Do you think your parents miss you?" I asked. We are at the same park Tiffany and I had a picnic at. I have a gut feeling I'm being set up. I'm experiencing too many coincidences between the two of them. Maybe getting caught would be a good thing for me. Maybe I'm more in love with the thrill. If I got caught I don't think I would go to Camille. Maybe I would. Would the feelings change? Here I go, putting my brain into thought overload.

"What made you ask me that? That was a very random question." At least we're not having a picnic. We're just walking through the park.

"I was just wondering. It's a critical part of your life. Do you ever think about them?"

"I rather not talk about them." You can see the annoyance on Camille's face.

"Why not?"

"They are the past. Who wants to live in the past? I have this process where I'm trying to be a better person each day. Each day has to be a day of me evolving as a person. I want my emotions and thoughts to evolve daily. To do that, I must forget about the past. I don't even think about yesterday's events. Keep moving forward, live in the moment. Never take the moment for granted. That's what I try to live my life by. Am I perfect at doing this? Of course not, but it's what I strive for."

"That's an interesting view to have on life." She nodded her head in agreement. I feel like she accidently avoided my question. No, she purposely avoided my question, but what can I do about it? I hate comparing the two, but with Tiffany I feel like she has no secrets. I feel like she reveals all her deepest thoughts to me, whether it's in my favor or not. I love that about her.

What am I doing here? I'm actually walking through the park with another woman. I'm acting like I have no significant other I could be spending time with.

"How do you feel about me?" Camille asked.

"I love you," I quickly replied.

"That's not telling me how you feel," she said with a smile. "That always seems to be your first reply to those types of questions. Someone asked me do I have a boyfriend. It weirded me out."

"Why was it weird to you?"

"Because I said yes." I wasn't expecting that for an answer, and I feel this thing we have has went to another level. I shouldn't have answered the phone earlier. Nooo, I had to think it would be a good idea for us to hang out today. The weird part is that I don't feel any anger. I'm not happy, but I'm not mad. What is going on with my feelings? She can't go around telling people I'm her boyfriend.

"Marcus, what are you thinking about?"

"I'm thinking about the reality that I'm getting married soon." There's silence in the air. I guess that's the underlying fact we both try to neglect. It's a reality. I'm getting married and won't call it off, even if I want to. Well, I don't want to, but am admitting that I'm confused and I'm not going to put in the effort to figure things out. I must go with the flow.

"What if I told her?" Camille asked.

"Told her what?"

"About us." My eyes just widened. I know, I just have to breathe. I want to lose my composure, but what will that accomplish?"

"Camille, Tiffany is the victim. She hasn't done anything to deserve what she's getting. I can't ruin the dream she's living in."

"Marcus, the dream she's living is a lie. Newsflash, you're in love with me. Okay, let's just say you are in love with her.

Would you really marry her knowing you're in love with two people?"

"I'll figure out a way to stop loving you."

"Marcus, shut up. I keep having to remind you of this. You've left me about four times. You always find your way back to me without me even trying. If you're going to leave, never come back. I'll figure out a way to move on. It's YOU that always rekindle what we have. Marcus, it's you. Admit it, you want what we have more than I do. And don't attempt to walk away like you always do when the conversation gets uncomfortable."

"I need time to think. If I come back, that will give you your answer." She shook her head.

"Or that could mean you're just back around with no answer. You're a master at leaving issues unresolved." I still haven't told her about my issues with my dad. How can I love someone I've barely opened up to? If that's the case, I should be in love with Christina, who may actually be my soul mate. At least she's not in denial about her craziness.

"Like I said, I need time to think. I also have an appointment I have to be at." I kissed her, turned around and walked away. My gut says to never come back. Too bad she knows I will. I may have another addiction.

"I think I'm going crazy. All these thoughts in my head, all these secrets I'm holding. I have an urge to change for the better, but there's a stronger urge. It's an urge of confusion. Is it possible to have feelings for someone when you can barely describe how you feel about yourself?"

"These secrets you hold, do they play a role in the confusion about yourself?"

"May I start bringing a bottle of liquor to our sessions?" I asked.

"Why would you want to do that?"

"I'm tired of attempting to be alone with my thoughts. I want the rest of my life to be a blur. Yes, I'm admitting to giving up on life. Life sucks, no matter how positive of an outlook I try to have on it."

"These secrets, would you like to reveal them?"

"Hell no, you're not about to judge me."

"I'm not allowed to judge you."

"Are you only that way at work? Is that also your life view? How are you once you leave work? You hear all these thoughts from different people, probably extreme thoughts. How do these thoughts affect you? I'm having suicidal thoughts. How does that make you feel?"

"Are you really experiencing suicidal thoughts?"

"No, I just wanted to see if it would change the tone in your voice. Your voice is always calm like you have everything under control. What bad situations are you going through? You're taking in people's darkest thoughts. How do you handle it? Do you find it weird that I've been coming here for a while and still haven't made eye contact during our conversations?"

"Which question would you like for me to answer first? Are you trying to turn into my therapist?" I burst out laughing.

"Do you need one? Or, since you're a therapist you feel like you've figured out everything? You know, I thought I could figure out everything on my own. I thought I had everything under control. It's amazing how quickly my life has spiraled out of control. It's like I blinked one time and my whole world had become one big disaster in motion."

"You have yet to mention the problems or secrets in your life." I shrugged my shoulders.

"I'll probably never tell you. I have a hard time opening up. The one person I could tell anything to is dead, which was my mom. That's the one person I truly loved with all my heart, and feels she loved me the same, if not more. How do I know that if I start opening up to you, the next day you won't die? Do you know how much that would crush me?"

"Your mom, when and how did she die? How are you coping with it?"

"She shouldn't be dead, I should. I mean that with all my heart. How dare God take her before me. All she did was spread love. All she received was hate and death in return. How in the fuck is that possible? What type of God or universe is running this thing we call life? How does my true love leave me here? Now I'm supposed to truly love another woman out here? Why? So she can die on me too?"

"When you speak of your mom, you almost speak of her in a tone that's stronger than a son/mother relationship."

"What love is stronger than motherly love? That bitch I'm forced to call a father left his true love to be with a man. Who's supposed to love her now? Me, it's my job. I'm all she had. I gave her all my love and still couldn't heal her pain. Fuck my dad. Fuck me for probably being able to do more but being distracted by a fiancé……." I stood up. "I've spoken too much, but at least you've did what others can't do. I'll see you again soon."

I got into my car. Wow, that was intense. I lost control of myself. I felt myself ready to cry. I can't come back here. I'm starting to get too comfortable. I need a drink.

****

"I think this was a great decision to move in together. I didn't think I would like it because I love my space. I now see that I'm wrong. I love living with you."

"I love living with you too."

"Do you really?" she asked. "Yes, I feel like you were sort of pressured into this decision by Christina." I'm now convinced that Tiffany knows I'm cheating on her. Her ability to read things is too good. I'm convinced she's waiting to see if I'm going to tell her. Even with that thought process, I know I'll truly be an idiot if I was to admit to my wrongdoings.

"Christina didn't pressure me into anything. I'm my own person, she's just influential," I smiled.

"You say you've been best friends since kids. Where has she been? How come I'm just meeting her? I know you're not lying about her, she knows too much about you."

"I'm still trying to figure out where she's been. About six years ago she vanished without warning. I went by her parents' home, they were also gone. I do know she's a totally different person now. I'm sure you can't notice it, but she really has some issues she's trying to figure out. I love her though, even if I don't know her anymore. She knows me better than a lot of people."

"Does she know you better than me?" Here's a situation where a lie would be bad, but the truth may be worse. How is that possible? How would Tiffany feel knowing she's my fiancé and doesn't know ten percent of the real me? Essentially, a stranger in her eyes knows me better.

"Of course not," I replied. "You're my fiancé, you know all of me." I kissed her on the lips. My life makes me wonder am I the only one? Am I the only person whose words and actions tell one thing, but thoughts tell something totally different when dealing with a significant other? I wish I knew of the person if they exist. Hopefully they're older than me and have been doing it for a long time. I would ask the person what was the end game. When your thoughts differentiate from your actions, where does that ultimately leave you?

"Do you ever think about kids?" Tiffany asked. I don't like where this is going.

"I don't," I quickly replied. "And that's only because you've told me multiple times you don't want any. The last time I gave you a signal I may want one, you shot the signal down."

"That was before accepting that we're engaged and finally moving in together," she said with a smile. "Moving in together confirmed that this is all real. Well, I'm going to get to work. I'll see you tonight." She kissed me on the lips and walked out the room. I just heard the front door shut. I opened my drawer and pulled out a bottle of Hennessy from under my clothes. Yes, I'm playing with fire, especially since Tiffany does the laundry. I really don't care anymore. It's time to get drunk and write this letter.

Dear Tiffany,

I have so many thoughts in my head, but don't know where to start. Could the liquor I'm drinking have an effect in this confusion? That's quite possible. Anyways, I desperately want to explain myself, but I'll just get to the point. It's over, we're over. I'm leaving you forever. My heart has been stolen by your friend, Camille. My heart has been stolen by her for a long time. The liquor is definitely having an effect on my brain. I can't even process the thoughts to explain how this happened. Or maybe I can, and it is just mind blowing to admit to myself. You deserve better. I've constantly lied to you. I take that back, our whole relationship is a lie, outside of the fact that I love you. The irony of that last statement. I've had unprotected sex with Camille and came back and had unprotected sex with you. My lips have touched yours after touching her lips. To make things worse, she's a transgender, and I've known about it. I've slept with her after finding out. I'm really drunk right now. What can I say? My feelings for her are stronger than they are for you. Fuck it, I said it. All the years, all the great memories, the wedding that's coming up, I'm throwing it all away for her. Yes, she's that important to me. I'm addicted to her. It's not fair to bring you along for ANOTHER addiction ride. Oh, I'm also addicted to liquor. I've been addicted to it long before you met me. You don't have to forgive me for it. I'm not asking for it.

Marcus

I should probably pack some clothes. I have no plans of coming back here.

"Marcus, I'm leaving," Camille said.

"No, you're not," I blurted out. Surprise is on her facial expression.

"Well, that wasn't the response I was expecting."

"Where are you going?"

"I'm going to California. I want to start over. Florida isn't the place for me. I'm learning that sometimes starting over is a good thing." My emotions are everywhere right now. I need to sit down and sort my thoughts out.

"You can't leave me here. Look at what we've built." I feel myself getting sad. I want to cry.

"Marcus, I never expected things to get to this point. I'm tired of being number two. I never planned on being in a scenario where I must be number two. It's funny how God seems to laugh at our plans."

"I left Tiffany." Her eyes widened. "I really did it."

"Why would you do that?" she asked. Did she just ask what I think she asked? I'm so confused right now.

"Because I want to be with you. I thought that was the plan, though we never said it."

"Marcus," she gently touched my face, "You're not ready to leave her yet. I see it in your eyes when you talk about her. I may bring a spark of happiness into your life, but you still love her. The eyes never lie. I'm not going to let you be with me until you're completely over her. It's not fair to either woman."

"But I've already left her. What am I supposed to do now?"

"You do what I've learned to do. Spend time with yourself. Take time to learn yourself." Well, this day isn't going exactly how I planned. The last time I spent time with myself, I was thinking of committing suicide. How have I lost my mom, my fiancé, and the other woman I love? Is it possible to lose everything? Is my luck really this bad? What have I done to deserve this?

"So, this is it? Are we officially done?" I asked.

"This may be a sign for both of us to soul search. You never know, maybe our souls will find a way back to each other." She walked away. Just like that, I'm right back at rock bottom. This is really rock bottom because now I have no one. What am I supposed to do now? The bottle seems to be my only loyal friend. Well friend, here I come.

****

"I thought of heavily relapsing, but seeing you in such a low state has me reconsidering my options."

"Christina, please don't start. Let me drink in peace."

"Marcus, you've been on my couch drinking for two consecutive days. I think it's now time for you to receive some input from me."

"Just watch me drink. No words, just watch." She shook her head. How dare she shake her head at me. Ok, so I've been drinking whiskey for two days, and I'm definitely drunk, but she still can't judge me. She has her own set of problems. We all are flawed.

"Where is Tiffany?" she asked.

"I've called her, she hasn't answered." I just realized that I haven't told Christina what's going on. She doesn't know I've called things off with Tiffany. She doesn't know the full situation with Camille. No wonder she has a look of confusion on her face. As far as she knows I'm just having a random episode of heavy drinking. In her opinion, it may be because of my mom.

"What's wrong? Tell me what's going on." My phone just rang. Shit, it's Tiffany. My heart is now beating fast. The effect of being drunk has quickly vanished. The easy way would be to run away from this situation. What will running solve?

"Hello," I slowly answered.

"Baby, oh my God. I'm so sorry. My grandmother had a stroke. When I received the call I immediately left work and rushed to the hospital. I left my phone at work because I was moving so fast. These past two days have been hectic. My grandmother didn't die, she will be fine, I think. I'm going to meet you at home in thirty minutes, Ok?" I quickly ended the call.

"I have to go," I said to Christina. I quickly stood up. Wow, the letter is still there. She hasn't been home to read it. If I make it home before her I can burn the letter. Take the 'if' away, I will make it home before her. Maybe there is a God. Maybe I'm not at rock bottom. Maybe this is my sign to go figure things out. I don't know what figuring things out consist of, but I do know I have to make it home to destroy that letter.

Yes, I beat her here. I was thirty minutes away but made it here in fifteen. I can now breathe a sigh of relief. Camille says she can see in my eyes that I still love Tiffany. Maybe she's right. I never stopped loving Tiffany, I just love Camille more. At least that's what I tell myself.

Yes, the letter is exactly where I left it. Luckily, I don't have any matches, otherwise I really would burn it. "Marcus," Tiffany said as she walked into the room, "What are you ripping up?" I honestly didn't hear the door open. I quickly balled up the rest of the letter and stuffed it in my pocket.

"Today, I'd actually written a letter telling you how much I missed you, since I hadn't heard from you in a couple of days," she smiled.

"You could have just sent me a text message. I didn't even have a missed call from you."

"I figured you may want a day or two to yourself. I've vanished on you before, so I'm totally understanding if you randomly want to do the same." She approached and hugged me. "I love you," I whispered into her ear.

"I love you too." Tiffany will never know how close we were from a life changing experience. It's funny how one moment can change everything. I've heard people say life is predestined; it's all one big plan. I'm starting to think differently. "May you make me something to eat while I take a shower?"

"Of course I will, baby." She walked into the bathroom. This makes me realize that I'm losing sight of the simple things. I used to make us breakfast and dinner at least three days a week. I haven't done this in months, without being conscious of it. I wonder has Tiffany noticed. She notices everything, why hasn't she mentioned it? She may think I'm grieving the death of my mom. Something like that can ruin a person for a very long time. Did Camille and I last so long because of all the events distracting Tiffany from the truth? In a perfect world would Tiffany have noticed my transgressions very early? I guess it's a good thing the world isn't perfect.

"Baby, us sitting at the dining room table has made me realize we haven't done this in a while, even before we moved in together. You even cooked my favorite meal." She smiled and chewed a piece of her chicken. I swear, it seems like all my thoughts come to light. It's that or Tiffany is a mind reader. Either way, I take it as a sign to stop thinking, especially if I haven't come up with an answer to my thoughts.

"Well love," I started, "If you stop being so busy, I'll have time to make us breakfast and dinner more often." She smiled and shook her head. "We have our best conversations while eating dinner. We must get things back to normal. I miss the moments."

"I agree, a hundred percent."

"How is your mom? How is the family?" I've learned to keep the conversation going when I feel Tiffany may think of a question I'm not ready for.

"My mom asked about you. She said she hasn't seen you in a while and misses her future son-in-law." She lifted her hand, referring to the ring. I assume she has told everyone, which I guess should have been expected. I'm the one who hasn't told anyone.

"Well, maybe we should go see your mom together." She smiled and nodded her head. Now that Camille is out the picture, I must learn how to be happy again.

Chapter 9

"You whispered Camille's name while you were sleep." Fear just leaped into my heart. Shit, how did this happen? This is exactly why I didn't want to move in together. Why would I be whispering her name? I didn't dream about her last night. The expression on Tiffany's face is a look of confusion and concern. I need to give her an explanation. I don't even have an explanation for this. My mind is trying to give me a reasonable excuse but none is forming. Even my mind is confused about this one.

"The rumor at work is Camille is about to get fired." A look of shock is on Tiffany's face. "I had a dream last night that it actually happened. I don't know why, but in the dream, I really felt bad for her. I'd even say I was sad, like I didn't want it to happen. I hate hearing that anyone is about to lose their job. In the dream, I was trying to stop it from happening. I was trying to be some type of hero."

"Why is she going to be fired?" Tiffany asked. "That's such horrible news. That has ruined my morning. I don't want to go to work now." Tiffany has a habit of feeling other's pain, literally. If someone she knows is sad, she automatically gets sad. Am I using that against her right now? Of course not, I'm not that horrible of a person. Or maybe I am.

"I believe the job is going in a different direction and they're making cuts. I can't confirm this is going to happen. It's just a heavy rumor at the moment. She hasn't been to work in the past three days. I'm not sure if she's heard the rumor or not."

"I should call her and check on her."

"Of course that would be your first thought, but what if she doesn't know? What if she's just on a vacation? I wouldn't want to put those thoughts into her head, especially if they aren't true. As far as I know it's just a rumor. It just happens to be a very loud rumor."

"I respect you for trying to stop it from happening in your dream. That was very sweet of you," she smiled.

"Hey, it was just a dream," I said with a smile. "That wouldn't happen in reality. I'm not doing that in the real world. We both will end up without a job. I think she's a pretty smart girl. If she's getting fired, she will find something new. It bothers me that I whispered her name in my sleep, even though she was in my dream. Why would I do that? That's so creepy."

"It's because you have a heart." If she only knew how right she was. I can't get away from her even if she's hundreds of miles away. I have to adjust back to a normal life. She's blocked my number, which lets me know she's serious. My chaotic life had become my new normal. Now that things are back to normal, life seems odd. I'm supposed to be happy but I'm not.

"Tiffany, I love you." She smiled and kissed me.

"I love you too, and always will." I believe her when she says that. People would give up a lot to experience unconditional love. Then there's me, a man who has it but feels like it may be from the wrong person. Maybe I'm wrong. Maybe Tiffany is the right person and has been the right person the entire time. I need to accept the fairytale ending and run with it. I cheated for months and didn't get caught. I need to go check on Christina.

"Marcus, I hate you!" I threw my hands up.

"What did I do? I haven't seen you in a week. How in the world do you hate me when I haven't talked to you? That makes no sense."

"You made me embarrass myself! I tried having sex with a dude. It was the most horrible experience ever!" I burst out laughing. "The shit is not funny! I feel like an idiot."

"What happened? He didn't get hard? Christina, is your vagina that bad?" I burst out laughing.

"Fuck you Marcus! He did get hard. What's the point in getting hard if the pussy isn't wet? We tried everything. He licked me EVERYWHERE, no positive result."

"What is wrong with your vagina?"

"Fuck you again Marcus!"

"Hey, I tried to give you the 800 for the hormone pills. You were the one acting like you're too good to take my money. I did my part."

"Marcus, I broke down and cried in front of him. It was so embarrassing. He thought it was his fault. I kept telling him it was my fault, which really had him confused. I couldn't tell him why. No one knows the reason why but you. You should have just licked my pussy when I asked you. You could have saved me the embarrassment!"

"I'm not licking that thing." She gave me the middle finger. "What did he say it tasted like? I really couldn't imagine licking that type of vagina. What, is it just dry down there?"

"Don't ask that like my pussy is some type of cardboard box." I burst out laughing. "Marcus, it's not funny. What am I going to do?"

"I still have the 800 if you want it. We can go to the bank right now." I stood up and grabbed my keys. I don't know how I'm going to explain an 800-dollar withdrawal to Tiffany. I will figure it out later.

"I don't want your money. Then you'll have something to hang over my head. Who knows when I'll be able to pay you back, if ever." I shook my head.

"What type of friend do you think I am? When have I ever done something for you and expected something in return?"

"Never, but if you knew what I've been through these past six years, you'd understand my resistance." She looked away. Something about her past is bothering her. I intend to find out, but know she may be more stubborn than me. She wasn't always this way.

"When are you going to let me know about your past?" I asked.

"Once you give me your reasoning for cheating on Tiffany," she replied. "I'll never forget your expression that day I saw her in your apartment. You can deny it all you want, that expression never lies. I think I may be a psychic."

"Could it be possible that she was just a friend? You've seemed to leave out that possibility." She shook her head. "So, you're convinced we had something stronger than a friendship?"

"Marcus, I know times have changed and we're not the same people, but you do know I was the person you could tell anything to, right? I know liquor has damaged your memory, but you have to remember that. You can't hold all the pain and secrets on the inside. It's inevitable that you lose your mind."

"This is the same woman who won't tell me about her past. Why haven't you gone crazy yet if that's the case?"

"Breaking news, I have gone crazy," she said in a sarcastic tone. "And I don't hold everything in. All I have to do is get readmitted into the psych ward. Some of the patients in there are my friends and hear all my problems. Even if I have to scream them because we're in separate padded rooms, they can hear me.

"Are you always in a padded room when you're there?"

"No, I'm with the patients during lunch. If you ever want to be understood, go to a psych ward for a few days." I scratched my head. Too much hair is growing on my head. I'm used to a low fade.

"Aren't the people in there crazy?" I asked.

"Marcus, we're all crazy," she bluntly replied. "Some of us are just better at admitting it to ourselves. Others believe the story they tell themselves. You keep telling yourself something, you'll eventually believe it, even if it's a lie. You should go there with me one day. You don't have to check yourself in, though you probably should," she burst out laughing, "You can meet some of the patients though."

"I'll pass on that offer. I may have a few issues, but not to that extent. My problems can easily be solved." She shook her head. Maybe her statement is true. Maybe I'm telling myself a story that sounds good in my head, but is a complete lie. Maybe I am borderline crazy but haven't crossed the line yet. No, I'm not crazy. I'm letting Christina play mind games with me.

"I can prove that you may be crazy." I burst out laughing. "I don't see what's so funny. I'm serious right now."

"Well, if you're so confident then prove it." I don't know what she has in mind, but she has my full attention. I've learned that you can't underestimate anyone's knowledge. Homeless people are some of the most knowledgeable individuals you'll come across. They just happened to make a few bad decisions along the way, which we all do."

"Marcus, forget it. I've just become sad. I miss my second mom. It seems like she's been in a coma for years and I still haven't been to the hospital to see her. I've found myself going through life with the assumption that she's already dead."

"That's a horrible assumption, but fine."

"Not being able to talk to her makes me feel guilty when I'm talking to my real parents. I haven't spoken to her in years and feel like I'm neglecting her. Anyways, who do you love more? Your mom or Tiffany?"

"My mom, of course. That's such a dumb question. I love you more than I love Tiffany." Her face is showing displeasure with my answer.

"You love me, but wouldn't lick my pussy to save me from a moment of embarrassment. Fool someone else with that. Anyways, assuming your mom dies, you would've lost a big part of you, a big part of your reasoning for living. How would you heal? What happens to those feelings? Do you even realize how much you love your mom? It's almost deeper than a mother/son relationship. You love her like a girlfriend, minus the sex." She sounds like my therapist.

"That's your observation. I don't think the love is that deep. I'm all she has. I have no choice but to love her. That's my responsibility. This is all pointless because we're being hypothetical. My mom is going to live."

"Marcus, you were probably too drunk to remember, but I was around you and her from the ages of six to seventeen. I saw the affection you had for her."

"Christina, what's your point?" I feel myself getting annoyed. I rarely get annoyed around Christina.

"A part of you would be dead, and you'd try to function like you're alive. I'm just going to say she is dead right now. She's dead until she wakes up. You're trying to go about loving Tiffany, when the only person you knew how to love is dead. You're messing with that other woman, pouring your feelings into her, when the person you cared about the most is dead. And you've convinced yourself that you can do it. Let me guess, you've taken a week to be away from everyone since she's been in a coma? Marcus, you've been internally damaged for a long time. You need much longer than a week. And that's what makes you crazy. You're a dead person on the inside trying to function. This is the type of stuff I learned while being in the psych ward."

"I'm not saying you're right, but what are you suggesting I do?"

"I'm suggesting you really heal. Forgive yourself first. I know you're blaming yourself for a lot of the bad that's occurred in your life. Go find your dad, forgive him for the hurt he's obviously caused in your life. I don't even have to know who he is, or what he did to know that it's affected you in a negative way. It forced you to love harder at a younger age than you needed to. Tell Tiffany you're cheating on her. You may need to soul search."

"First, I don't know how you've convinced yourself I'm cheating on Tiffany. That was just a friend, a friend who I don't speak to anymore. Second, I've already found my dad and hate him more than I used to."

"Marcus, you really don't tell me anything while I tell you EVERYTHING. I don't know what type of friendship this is. You have too many secrets for us to truly be best friends." She shook her head. She's right about that. I do have secrets, secrets I wish I didn't have, and she knows everything though I haven't told her yet. Maybe I do need to heal. Maybe I am a dead person on the inside trying to function. Maybe I really am crazy and have been in denial about it.

****

"Marcus, have you made a list of who you'd like to be in our wedding?" Tiffany asked. It's been a month since Christina and I have had that conversation, and I still haven't made any changes. The conversation has stayed on my mind. I've actually gone a whole month without talking to Camille. I'm doing what I thought couldn't be done, only because she's given me no other options. I've called her every seven days while hoping she's taken me off the block list.

"No, I haven't. I'll come up with names soon."

"Mister, you're the one that proposed to me. Why am I more excited than you?" she asked with a smile. "I thought you planned all this out while you were in jail." I took a deep breath.

"A lot has happened since I spent those few days in jail. I sometimes wish I would have stayed in there for a little while longer. You know what? Forget those last statements. I need to focus."

"Marcus, are you thinking of breaking off the wedding? Please tell me now. Don't wait till the actual wedding day like they do on the movies. I will be able to accept it if you want to have a change of heart. I will be upset, but at least you're saving me the embarrassment." She cares about me. She's giving me a way out. She's giving me what I want.

"Why would I break off the wedding? We've come this far, we can't back out now." Great, she gives me a genuine way out and I don't take it. What is wrong with me? Am I really as crazy as Christina says I am?

"I'm just making sure. I wanted to give you a way out, just in case you were having second thoughts. I can't read your mind, so I have to ask things to see where you're at mentally. I have to remind myself that I can't relate to the situation you're going through. I don't know the healing process or how long it takes."

"I think I need to go on a soul-searching journey." Would I be able to live with myself if I married Tiffany without letting her know the real me? I have a conscience, though I try to convince myself I don't. I still care about sleeping peacefully at night. That has not been the case these past few months. I can at least tell her about my alcoholism.

"What does a soul-searching journey consist of?" she asked. Here she goes, asking questions I don't have the answer to. I expect her to just agree, though I should know better. Is soul-searching just a way of finding yourself? If I give that as an answer, that'll just open up more questions. She'll then be able to say we are together as a couple to help each other find ourselves. That's supposed to be a part of the journey. Let me breathe, I feel myself thinking too much.

"I take back the soul-searching journey. I just need to refocus my thoughts. Let me get focused on this wedding. This is going to be the happiest day of our lives. I'm putting the past behind me. I'm tired of living in the past. It isn't healthy."

"Do you want your dad to be in the wedding?" she asked. The question has put me into deep thought. It's a question I've asked myself. Part of me wants to forgive him, the other part blames him for everything, literally. I identify more with the latter part, which means I still have hate in my heart. I want to start a new relationship with him, then I think to myself that we've never had a relationship.

"Put him on the list," I replied. "I'm going to attempt to rekindle things with him again."

"Again?" she asked. "You tried to rekindle the relationship with your dad? Where was I when this happened?" Great, I thought it was her I'd told about our day at Starbucks, but it was actually Camille. I can't distinguish the moments between the two. It's hard because I was experiencing special moments between the two in close spans. "You mentioned seeing him at the hospital and it not being a great experience. I had no clue you saw him again after that day. I didn't know you tried to work on the relationship."

"Please forgive me for not telling you about that day. I probably didn't tell you because it was a quick, forgetful scene. Maybe I'm the one to blame. I had a lot of hate in my heart. I'm trying to open my heart to accepting things and letting go of the past. Maybe seeing him again will be a better experience."

"Maybe you should let me go with you. I can be by your side. When you get that urge to get up and walk away, I'll be around to make you stay. Like I said, he's the only parent you have now."

"I have no parents." Her face has saddened. "You don't have to go with me, I won't walk away if things go wrong, I promise." She smiled and grabbed my hand. I really don't want to do this, but don't want to stay stagnant in my thought process. I need to call Christina and make sure she's fine. I may be over exaggerating, but I imagine me calling her and learning that one of her voices have told her to do something very damaging. I hope she answers the phone.

"Hello," she calmly answered.

"Christina, what are you doing?"

"Watching porn," she bluntly replied. "What are you doing?"

"Whoa, wait a minute. You answered the phone while watching porn? Who does that? I know it's normal, but it's weird talking to you while you're watching porn. I feel uncomfortable." I have a feeling she's over there shaking her head.

"Would you rather me be popping pills? I really thought about it. I'm clinically diagnosed with mental complications. It's easy to get my hands on prescribed pills, the legal way." She burst out laughing. I honestly don't see what's funny.

"Please, don't use any pills you don't need."

"Hey, I can become a drug dealer! I never thought about that! I'm quitting my job tomorrow! It's time to make some real money."

"Christina, you're not selling pills. When did you get a job? Have you been working since we reconnected at the park?" Great, I hear the moans from the porn in the background.

"Shit, this porn is having no type of an effect on me! I just want to get wet. I'm not asking for too much!" I think she's forgotten that I'm on the phone. "Oh shit, Marcus? What were we talking about? No, I remember now. Yes, I've been working, though it's part-time and at a shitty place. When I go on my psych ward field trips for a few days, they always allow me to come back. I can never complain."

"I didn't know that."

"I would go crazy if I didn't have a job. Spending time with my voices all day would drive me insane, if I'm not insane already. That would be torture! Hey, my mom is calling me. I'm going to call you back." The call ended. Well, at least I know she's doing good.

****

My dad invited me to his home when I offered a second chance at meeting up. I declined off first instinct, then became too stubborn to change my mind. I suggested the same Starbucks we met at the first time, but am hoping for a different outcome. He agreed, so now I sit at one of the tables and wait. I'm twenty minutes early and should have brought my laptop to avoid looking so awkward while sitting here.

He's just walked in. Wonderful, he brought his significant other and younger son with him. I feel myself getting angry. No, I don't want to breathe. Why did he bring them? I should get up and leave while they're in line getting their coffee. I'm now annoyed and don't want to hide it. I hear my mom's voice telling me it's always good to be the bigger person. Maybe I don't want to be the bigger person right now.

"Son," he happily started as him and the others sat down, "I'm happy we decided to try this again." There's so many negative words I want to say right now. I want to tell him that I wanted US to try this again, not THEM. I want to tell him that I hate him, and seeing his family will forever leave a hole in my heart. I won't close the hole even if I could.

"Yeah, the last time didn't go as planned." I took a sip from my coffee. "I would like for you to be in my wedding." His eyes just lit with excitement. The smile I'm placing is forced. I should soften my heart, but am learning that a softened heart leaves you open to more hurt.

"I would love to be in your wedding. I can't wait to meet your fiancé. Would it be asking too much to suggest that they be in the wedding also?" He pointed at the other two. Is he fucking serious? My first reaction is to get up and walk out. He's lucky I promised Tiffany I wouldn't do it. How do you offer the family you left me for to be in MY wedding? Does he not understand any of the pain he's put me through?

"Sure, they can be in the wedding," I said. "I need more men anyway. This will save me the trouble of asking other people." He smiled and nodded his head.

"How are you handling your mom's death?"

"How are you handling it?" I asked back. He took a sip from his coffee. He seems to be thinking about his answer. I'm assuming the wrong answer could upset his significant other. I just realized that now I have to get to know all three of them. Getting to know my dad is going to be tough enough. I honestly had no intentions of knowing his family. They took him away from me, I'm not supposed to want to know them.

"Well, I was at the funeral. I was somewhere you wasn't. May I ask why?" I looked away. No, he may not ask why. I should be asking why. I should be asking why to everything. Am I being selfish right now? If I am, I feel like I've earned the right to be. I've been through enough. His significant other is closely paying attention. He reminds me a lot of the actor Omar Epps, just a shade lighter.

"I chose not to go. I couldn't do it. I don't know if you can relate to what it feels like, but once I received the phone call, I'd never felt more alone at that moment. My dad had left me, and at that moment I felt like my mom had done the same. Let's just say I wanted to get adjusted to being in that moment. I wanted to get used to the permanent lonely feeling."

"Son, I don't know what to say." He looks like he's about to cry.

"Do you miss her?" The little boy asked. My heart tells me it would be wrong to be angry at him. He's only eight. He had no control over any of this. He's an innocent bystander in my opinion. I guess I'm more jealous because he's receiving the love I wanted.

"I miss her more than anyone will ever understand." I switched my eyes back to my dad. "Would you have come back around if Mom was never in the hospital? How did you find out?"

"I knew one of the nurses at the hospital that noticed her and decided to give me a call. I had no other option but to come see her."

"Are you going to avoid my first question?"

"Let's focus on the wedding," he replied. He took a sip from his coffee. What in the hell does that mean? My head is going to explode from all these thoughts I want to lash out but am being forced to keep in my head. Why am I even here? God knew what he was doing when he put it in my mind to meet back here at Starbucks. If we were at his house, I doubt I'd be as friendly. I'm almost certain I wouldn't be.

"Well, we've established that you're going to be in the wedding. I'll send you the other information via text or phone call. We are still trying to figure everything out." I stood up and walked out of Starbucks. I don't think it would be a bad thing if I never saw him again. He's not the man I remember.

"Well, how did it go?" Tiffany excitedly asked as I walked into the house. My guess is she's been sitting on the couch waiting for me to come in.

"Do you want the lie or the truth? I asked. She's displaying a look of confusion.

"What type of question is that? Why would I want a lie? You've never lied to me before. This will not be the first."

"Well, he agreed to be in the wedding." She smiled, showing all her teeth. "Him and his family." Her eyes just lit up with excitement. Her hopes of this wedding are finally coming together.

"Wow, he brought his girlfriend or wife? They also have a child that will be in the wedding? This is great news. Is the child a son or daughter?" Great, Tiffany doesn't know the story behind my dad. I believe I told her he left when I was two or three.

"My dad's significant other is a man. They adopted a son that is now eight years old. I'm not sure when they adopted him." Tiffany's expression has gone blank. "You look like you just saw a ghost." I burst out laughing.

"That statement took me by surprise. I can't wait to meet them." I want to tell her that my dad is an arrogant, inconsiderate piece of shit, but that may be too harsh. Maybe I should keep my opinions to myself. There will be no relationship building with that man. After the wedding, I never want to see him again. I wonder if my mom approves of my decisions. Would she want him in the wedding if she were alive? There's so many questions I want to ask him.

"He's an interesting person, to say the least." I'm just realizing that Tiffany has a new hairstyle. She cut all her hair off, wow. How long has it been this way? I'm scared to ask, with the fear that it's been this way for a while and I'm just noticing. I used to notice and compliment her on the little things. "Baby, have I changed?"

"What do you mean?" she asked back.

"I don't know how to word the question differently. How about this, have I changed as a person over this past year? And don't tell me everyone changes. I know we all evolve as people. I know you're going to try to give me a scientific answer." I burst out laughing.

"You've changed in more ways than you probably have noticed. You started changing before your mother died. You've obviously changed since she's died. You're not the same Marcus I met years ago, but it may be selfish on my part to still want you to be that person. I just adjust and learn. I know you still have the same heart and still love me. That's all that matters at the end of the day."

"How have I changed?" I may be asking a question I really don't want the answer to. If she's truthful, she's going to say a bunch of bad things, which is going to upset me and force me to think about Camille. I feel I may be asking to be put in a negative state of mind. I may need to call Christina and tell her to check me into that psych ward. What is wrong with me?

"Do you really want to know?" she asked.

"Not really," I quickly replied.

"Well, I'm going to tell you anyway." I nodded my head. I can't get upset, I asked for this. "You've become more distant in the past year like you don't want the relationship to proceed, but sex me like you never want me to leave. It used to be the opposite. There was that moment where you were overly passionate, where I thought you were maybe seeing me as someone else while having sex with me. That person is gone. You're telling me a different sex story now."

"Sex story?"

"We tell each other stories every time we have sex with our energies. It's my job to read the story and figure out what you're trying to tell me. Your story pattern has changed, even becoming conflicting at times." Shit, she knows. She knows that I've cheated on her.

"My patterns have become conflicting? How?"

"For a period, I had trouble reading what you were trying to tell me. Sometimes it felt like you were telling me you didn't want to be on top of me, you actually wanted to be on top of someone else. The sex was….. weird. Usually when we're done I feel refreshed. For that period, I used to feel empty after sex, then started asking myself was it me. Was I doing something wrong is what I was asking myself."

"How am I supposed to respond to that?" I wonder am I sweating as hard on the outside as I am on the inside. I really have no words to respond to her interpretation. I've always liked Tiffany because she seemed to vibrate on a higher frequency. I guess I wasn't aware of how high she was vibrating. I've been telling her I was cheating the whole time and didn't realize it.

"I'm not sure how you respond to it. Your story patterns have gone back to normal. The change started before your mom died, then changed again after she died, but you're back."

"Would you have told me this if I'd never asked?" She looked at the ceiling.

"Well, I did ask you were you visualizing someone else while making love to me. Would I've come to you with this much detail? Probably not. I express my feelings about it in my paintings. Painting is the best way to express myself when I feel like I have no one to talk to." I nodded my head. I don't know why I'm nodding my head. Maybe this is my reality check to never disrespect Tiffany again.

Chapter 10

"Marcus, do you ever just want to die?" Christina asked. I call to check on her and this is the first question she asks me.

"Do you need for me to come over there?"

"I've been thinking about death a lot lately. Bryan tells me death may not be such a bad thing. It will put my mind at ease. He said he doesn't want to lose his best friend though. It made me realize I don't want to lose Bryan. I can't lose my best friend. His voice soothes me. Death sounds good though."

"Christina, you can't die. I need you to be in my wedding." She just mumbled something.

"Marcus, how in the hell do I mention death and we somehow get to YOUR wedding? What a narcissist!" I burst out laughing. I thought me mentioning my wedding would make her want to live. Maybe seeing me get married would inspire her to get married. "But OK, I'll die after your wedding. You have to speak at my funeral."

"Christina, I didn't go to my own mom's funeral. There's no way I'm going to yours?" She gasped.

"Your mom died?"

"She's been dead for a while now. Where have you been?" She's mumbling something else. My guess is these aren't happy words. I'm just realizing I never told her my mom died. I should have told her when she was giving me those assumptions. Everything has happened so fast. I'm a really horrible friend.

"Marcus, why didn't you tell me?" she angrily asked. "This entire time I thought she was still in a coma. Fuck you, Marcus!" The call ended. Wow, she really hung up on me. I guess I deserved that. I want to call her back, but what's the point? All she's going to do is curse me out. She loved my mom. She's about to go through that same phase I went through, great. I must go see her.

Great, she's changed her locks. My key is worthless now. Why would Christina change her locks? She has no stalkers. "Open up," I hollered as I knocked on the door.

"Marcus, leave me the fuck alone!" She screamed from the inside. She must be in the living room. "My second mom is dead and I had no clue because of you! I mentioned the thought of her being dead and you said nothing! I'm about to pop these pills with some liquor and have myself a pity party. Go back and do whatever you were doing to make you forget to tell me my second mom is dead. Hold on, Julie! I'm coming!"

"Who in the hell is Julie?"

"That's my suicide voice's name." I knocked on the door harder. "Marcus, I'm right here. Stop knocking on the door! I'm not going to answer it. Go away, leave me alone, let me suffer in peace. I knew I should have went to the hospital that day. You promised me she would wake up!"

"Christina, please open the door." Now that I'm on the other side of the coin, it makes me wonder if I was acting this way. I mean, I was alone during the process, but would I have reacted this way if the roles were reversed? Now that I think about it, this is exactly how I was acting, maybe worse. Maybe I should leave her alone. Loneliness is all I wanted during that period.

"Marcus, I'm not going to kill myself, I promise."

"I don't believe you."

"That's good, you shouldn't believe me. I just want to be left alone. Let me be alone with my thoughts." I may already know her answer to my next comment. I still must say it.

"Christina, I don't trust you alone with your thoughts at a time like this. You can call me a narcissist all you want. I'm not going anywhere until you open the door. I'll sleep outside on this porch. I'm not leaving you alone here." Great, it just started showering with rain. I guess I better get comfortable.

Four hours have passed and it's still raining. I'm still sitting on the floor mat, in front of the door, soaking in rainwater. She's still in there crying and screaming. She hasn't stopped in four hours. I already texted Tiffany and told her I'm not coming home tonight. At least my reason is good this time.

"Marcus, are you crazy?" I opened my eyes. I'm soaking wet, literally. I didn't even know I fell asleep. What time is it? How long was I sleeping? I'm happy to see that Christina is still alive. I really fell asleep on her. I now feel guilty. If she would have committed suicide I would have never forgiven myself. "Why did you sleep out here?"

"I wanted to keep you safe." I stood up. Christina looks like she hasn't slept yet. I wonder how long she was crying for. "May I come in and change my clothes?"

"Marcus, I'm not your mistress. You have no clothes here." I shook my head. "And no, you can't come in here. You need to go home to your fiancé and explain why you're soaking wet and didn't come home yesterday. If she decides she doesn't want to marry you, it's not my fault. I'm still upset with you."

"I understand."

"No, I don't think you do. I haven't been to sleep yet. After all that crying and screaming, it seems like all my voices started talking to me at once. It was torture at the highest degree. I eventually started screaming and trying to punch the voices, so in reality I was punching myself. It's all your fault, Marcus. I never got to see my second mom again. It's going to torture me for years, maybe forever."

"You will eventually get over it. Pain heals with time." She shook her head.

"I don't think you know who you're talking to. I can hold on to pain for a long time, till the point that I mistake pain for pleasure. You don't know all the pain I'm holding in. I'm thinking of getting tattoos. I hear that could help with my addiction to pain on a psychological level. It wasn't from a professional. A friend told me that."

"I don't have any tattoos. I don't know if that's true or not." I looked down. "Let me get home to my fiancé. I need to think of my truth to tell her, though it's going to sound like a lie, which is understandable."

"I'm probably going to get drunk when you leave. Before you get upset, please know I promise to be safe." I walked away. I want to stand there and argue with her, but what's the point? I have to get back to Tiffany. All I can do is hope for the best with Christina.

I pulled up to our home. This feels awkward, which is a reality check to how much I've been lying lately. I feel guilty, when in reality I haven't done anything wrong. I guess this is the side effect of being a habitual cheater. Cheating is like a drug, and I overdosed on that drug. Am I supposed to go in here and apologize? I was trying to save a friend from doing harm to herself.

"Why are you soaking in water?" Tiffany asked as I walked into the house. I immediately stripped down, leaving my clothes in front of the door. I'll probably throw the clothes away. I'm now completely naked.

"I had a long day and night." I truthfully replied. Being naked has made me think about Camille and how she loved seeing me this way. I must shake away the thought before I become erect. That would cause a whole bunch of problems I don't need right now. This is not the time to try to get the mood right.

"Well, that's telling me a lot. I received your text. I texted you back asking is everything okay, but received no response." I took a deep breath. Why am I scared of telling the truth? This is mind boggling to me.

"I didn't realize I hadn't told Christina about my mom's death. I'll just say she didn't take it well. My mom was like her second mom. The last she'd heard was that Mom was in the hospital. Mom has been dead for months and she's just finding out. She had a mental breakdown and blamed me for everything. To make sure she didn't do anything crazy, I went over there. She didn't let me in so I waited outside until she decided to."

"Did she ever let you in?" Tiffany asked.

"Nope." I shook my head. "I ended up sleeping on her front porch, trying to listen from the door to make sure she's okay. I fell asleep. I let her down." Tiffany's eyes widened.

"Is she dead?"

"Oh no, but she could have died. Sleep must have been more important to me. I'm beating myself up over it on a mental level. I really just want to sleep. Right when I thought I was finally accepting my mom being dead, I get this. Now it's replaying in my head all over again. She's not going to be at the wedding." I feel the tears forming in my eyes. Tiffany walked over and hugged me.

"Marcus, it's going to be okay."

"What if it's not? What if I never get over it? What if I'm effected forever. What if the nightmares come back now that I'm thinking about it again?"

"Marcus, we must be positive about it. You may need a new release. I'm not referring to a book. You should start painting with me."

"I'm not artistic at all. I wouldn't be able to paint a straight line if you offered me a million dollars." She burst out laughing.

"Baby, it's not about being artistic, it's about expression. You just let however you're feeling do the work. You don't have to be the next Picasso." I just realized I'm still naked.

"All of my art is going to be dark. I don't want people thinking I'm this miserable person walking around every day. I want to….. I don't want people to see my reality." She gently rubbed my face.

"Baby, who said that anyone had to see it? I have plenty of paintings I show no one, including you. And you are in a dark place. There's nothing wrong with that. We all go through dark periods in life."

"I don't think I've ever seen you in a dark period before, Tiffany. You're always positive, always upbeat. Even when you're in a tough situation, you always have the right attitude when trying to figure things out. Honestly, the only times I've seen you get extremely upset is when I displayed abnormal actions because of my mom's death."

"When you didn't go to the funeral, didn't come home, and wasn't answering your phone, that put me in a very dark place. It left me in a state of confusion. I was asking myself questions I'd never asked before. It made me realize how lonely I am without you. Yes, I have friends, but none of them have a piece of me spiritually like you do."

"Is this your way of trying to make me feel bad?" I asked with a smile. "Wait a minute. How did we get on this topic? We went from talking about me painting to talking about you being lonely and in a dark place. Let's get back on topic." She burst out laughing.

"So, are you interested in painting to express yourself?" I nodded my head. What's the worst that can happen besides me not liking it? I'm actually quite nervous, just because I'm stepping into the unknown. How will my work turn out? I may learn something new about myself, and who's to say that's a good thing? I guess I will find out soon.

****

I think I may be getting over Camille. I deleted her number out my phone. Before that, I'd outgrown the habit of calling her once a week. Out of sight, out of mind. I've slowly but surely stopped thinking about her. I'm only thinking about her now because I realized nothing happens when she comes to my mind. There's no urge, no emotion. I deserve a pat on the back.

The front door opened. Wow, I never sit alone on this couch. I've just been sitting here, daydreaming. "Baby, I made a mistake," Tiffany said as she closed the front door. "Camille kissed me."

"What?" I asked. I think my heart has stopped beating. Did I hear her correctly? There's no way she said what I think she said. I still must be daydreaming.

"Camille kissed me." Tiffany looks like she's in a state of shock. I'm so confused right now. "And I think I liked it."

"When did she come back!"

"How did you know she was gone?"

"Hold on, did you say she kissed you? Did you say you liked it?" Tiffany frowned and looked down. I stood up. I can't explain how I'm feeling right now.

"May I sit down?" Tiffany asked. "I need to get my thoughts together." She walked over and sat down on the couch. I'm still standing up. There are too many thoughts going through my head right now. "Marcus, what happened?"

"That's what I'm trying to find out!" I angrily replied. I sat down by her. "I'm sorry for raising my voice." I took a deep breath. "Now, may you please explain to me what happened?" She wiped her tears away.

"Do you want the long or short version?" I'm trying hard to stay calm.

"How did the two of you end up kissing?" She looked away. I hate when she looks away from me during our conversations. It really irritates me.

"I don't know. It just kind of happened." OK, I'm officially annoyed now.

"Give me the long version."

"Marcus, does this make me a cheater? I kissed another woman and liked it. I didn't want to stop. I've never even viewed women in that way. Her lips were so soft. Her tongue was...."

"Whoa, wait a minute. You had your tongue in her mouth?" Tiffany looked away. "Tiffany, look at me. I'm trying to have a conversation with you." I'm trying to fight off the state of shock I'm in. How did this happen?

"Her hands are so gentle. The way they gripped my ass when she pulled me in to kiss. Marcus, I'm sorry for doing it, but I don't regret the moment. I loved it. What is wrong with me? I've never cheated before. I don't know how to handle all of this. I'm so confused right now. What happens with us? Are you going to leave me?" I think I need to vomit.

"I think I'm going to faint."

"Marcus! No, you can't faint. I need you in the moment. I need you to help me understand this. You're the shoulder I have to lean on." I feel myself getting light headed. I think I need to lie down. No, I can't pass out. I must stay strong and figure this out. What in the hell is happening with my life?

"May I take a nap and act like this never happened when I wake up?" Tiffany threw her hands up. I've never seen Tiffany like this before. She's really freaking out.

"Marcus, what in the hell is that going to do for the reality we're living in?" I stood up, walked to our room, closed the door and locked it. It feels like my world is caving in. Where is my pen and tablet? I can't leave all these thoughts in my head.

Dear Diary,

My first thought was to run out and go get a bottle of liquor. I quickly had to override that thought. I've been telling myself I'm controlling my alcohol addiction. Diary, maybe talking to you will help me put things in perspective. How does the woman I cheated on my fiancé with (who also used to be a man supposedly) get my fiancé to cheat on me with her? Diary, how? She still hasn't told me what happened, but has admitted that she liked it. Is that a normal thing to do? Am I supposed to automatically stay with her because she admitted her wrongdoings to me? At least she kissed a girl, right? I'm so confused right now. I cheated on her with the same person. Diary, how do I make sense of it all? Or maybe it's not supposed to make sense.

Marcus

"Marcus, open the door!" I quickly put the tablet and pen in my drawer. How long has she been knocking? I really zoned out while writing. I'm still confused, but feel a little bit better. I opened the door. "Marcus, what the fuck? You can't lock me out of my own room. I'm your fiancé!"

"Wow, I've never heard you say that curse word before." She looks like she wants to punch me in the face right now. You can see it in her eyes. If my life was a book, this would be a major plot twist.

"Marcus, what are we doing? What's going to happen to us? I feel like I've steered our relationship onto an unknown path. Marcus, it's all my fault."

"Nothing is going to happen to us. We're going to move forward. It's the only thing we can do."

"Marcus, why don't you seem upset anymore?" she sadly asked. "What changed once you walked into this room? What thoughts are going through that head of yours? I need solutions, not just answers." I took a deep breath. I need to go into a separate room and meditate for an hour. I hear the bar calling my name. I'm not going to come up with any answers while being in this house.

"Tiffany, what would you like to do?" I calmly asked. I guess my suggestion of moving forward wasn't enough of a solution. If it was up to me, we'd move on and I'd figure it out while we're moving. Sitting here trying to figure it out piece by piece is going to fry my brain.

"I want to see Camille again," she replied. I feel my blood boiling. That's not the answer I was expecting. "We only kissed, but I'd be lying if I didn't admit that I want to experience more. I want to feel her on top of me. I want to experience what story her energy tells. I think we had a spiritual connection." My facial expression is blank.

"Tiffany, I'm going to head to the bar now and overdose on liquor. I can't guarantee that I'm going to make it back home. Go do whatever you feel like doing." Where are my keys? I need to leave this place NOW!

"Marcus, what is that going to solve? Running away from this situation isn't going to solve it. I'm trying to be a real woman about the situation and talk to you. The first thing you want to do when something doesn't go your way is walk away from the problem."

"Go be with Camille. You've admitted you have the urge. I'm not going to stop you. The wedding is off. Go be happy. What? Is that what you want to hear? Go experiment with girls and life. It may be more than just a phase, it may be a part of you." I grabbed my keys. I'm pretty sure I'm going to cry in the car.

"I haven't even told you what happened!" I put on my hat. It's time to tune everything out. How my life has arrived to this point will never make sense to me, even if God himself explained it to me. Life was close to perfect about a year ago. Wow, my birthday is tomorrow. This is one hell of a birthday gift. "Marcus, talk to me."

"I rather not." I put on my jacket. I'm not even sure if it's cold outside. I just want to wear a leather jacket.

"Marcus, Camille has a unique energy. She knows how to comfort a person. She knows how to soothe a person's soul. She's a great listener and knows how to make you feel like you're in the center of her universe. She caught me at a very vulnerable moment during our conversation. I needed clarity. I needed advice from a person on the outside that's not family. She hugged me and whispered in my ear that everything will be alright. Hugging her made me feel a sense of completeness."

"And let me guess, you caught eye contact with her when backing away from the embrace? Her eyes told you some type of story, a story that signified that the hug may have meant more than a friendly hug. The energy surrounding the two of you were strong. The energy was doing all the talking, while the two of you were actually silent while staring in each other's eyes."

"Wait, how did you know that? How did you describe the scene perfectly? Have you talked to Camille?" I shook my head.

"I'm probably the last person Camille wants to be in contact with right now. It sounds like a fairytale movie, which is something I could imagine you falling for. I believe what we have is more of a reality. The fairytale is something fresh, something new, so go follow it. I'm not stopping you. I'll be back to pack my belongings, just in case the fairytale leads you to believing she should move in."

"Marcus....." I walked out of the room. There's nothing else to say. I can't even explain the emotion I'm experiencing at the moment. It's more like a numbness. I planned on crying while in the car but what's the point? Crying isn't going to change anything. There's nothing that a few bottles of liquor can't solve.

"Marcus, what in the hell are you doing on my porch?" Christina asked. "You didn't knock or ring the doorbell. Are you drunk?" I opened my eyes. Wow, I honestly don't know how I ended up on her porch. I don't remember driving here. The last thing I remember is leaving my house and going to the liquor store.

"Don't mind me," I slowly slurred. "Just let me sit here in peace and enjoy this major headache I have right now." It's still nighttime and I'm assuming I haven't been here that long. "What time is it? This is a major headache I have." I looked to my right. There's an empty bottle of whiskey beside me. I need to sleep this headache away.

"Why are you not at home?" Christina asked with concern in her voice. I see she now has a tattoo of cursive writing on her forearm. It's too small to read from a distance. Maybe I should get tattoos. Too bad I'm terrified of needles. For some reason, they remind me of junkies.

"I have no home," I truthfully replied. "If you don't mind, I'd like to make this porch my home. I don't need any bathroom for a shower. I'll even pay you rent." I thought I was at rock bottom before, now I know there's another level under rock bottom. Wow, I'm really homeless. The worst-case scenario is I end up sleeping in my car until I figure things out, assuming I start to figure things out.

"Marcus, what are you talking about? Cleary, you're drunk right now. Come inside and I'll make you some coffee. We can get to figuring out what's going on in that head of yours." I want to get up but my legs feel stuck. Yes, I'm absolutely drunk right now. How do you wake up drunk? I must have been drinking heavy before passing out. Can coffee cure a headache? Coffee and headaches don't seem like they'll have a good relationship together.

"Christina, my legs are literally stuck to the ground. Now, if you wouldn't mind picking me up and taking me into your house, I'd gladly appreciate it. By the way, do you still need that sexual favor?" Christina shook her head.

"Now that I think about it, you coming into my house may not be a good idea. You're clearly too drunk to think. I'll see you in the morning." She walked into the house and closed the door. I guess I should get comfortable.

"Marcus, you have to talk to me." I guess she's forgotten the fact she made me sleep outside last night. The first time I slept on the porch was totally understandable. Last night was just wrong on her part. It was cold last night. She could have at least given me a blanket, though I did have my jacket. Now she wants me to talk to her. Why should I? I guess I need to talk because I need somewhere warm to stay. I could sleep in my car but Florida is experiencing chilly weather at the moment.

"Tiffany is gay," I bluntly stated. Christina gasped and covered her mouth with her hand. Wow, I actually said it aloud. It sounds worse saying it aloud. I should have kept the truth inside my mind. "She's kissed a woman and have caught feelings. That woman...." I almost said too much. I need to leave out who the woman is. "She now wants to have sexual intercourse with the woman."

"How does that make you feel?" Christina asked. I was hoping she wouldn't ask me this. I don't want anyone asking me this question.

"I feel like I'm in a horrible relationship with karma. I feel defeated. Tiffany and I were supposed to get married. We've been planning it! I feel like I've failed as a boyfriend and fiancé. I'll even admit that I'm depressed. It totally surprised me. Maybe it's my ego. A woman taking my woman is crushing."

"Do you want her back?" Her question has put me into deep thought. I haven't given this question any time to think on. I went directly to the liquor. I wish I could tell Christina the entire story. I want to call my therapist, but I'm still upset at his abilities. He got me to expose parts of myself I wanted to keep concealed. I'll probably never go back to visit him.

"I planned on marrying this woman, of course I want her back. This is the woman I planned on spending the rest of my life with. I don't want to throw all these years away." What's amazing is that a few months ago I was truly willing to throw everything away. My life in the past year could be a movie. I feel myself getting upset. This is all Camille's fault. She's ruined my life from all angles. I should have stayed on the path I was on.

"You should attempt to get her back," Christina stated. "If what the two of you had is real, there's no way the feelings are gone that quickly. Any feelings she may have for that woman can't be stronger than the feelings she has for you. It's not possible, unless she's known this woman for a very long time and those feelings have always been there." I stood up. Christina has a point. I may be able to fix this.

I opened the door to our home. All I can do is stare. Tiffany is naked, eyes closed, legs up and spread apart, with Camille's face in between, on the couch we always sit on. I should probably turn around and go get back into my car, but I won't. I've been running from everything. I'm going to stand here and accept defeat, accept the humiliation to my ego. I haven't been gone for two days and Tiffany has already started exploring her sexual confusions, and seems to be loving it. Tiffany opened her eyes and looked in my direction.

"Oh my God," she said as she pushed Camille's face away. Camille quickly looked in my direction. Fear is now in her eyes. She quickly stood up. "Marcus, what are you doing here? I didn't hear the door open." Tiffany stood up. I wonder what my mom is saying from heaven right now. She's probably saying what I'm telling myself, that I probably deserve this. Why do I deserve this? I'm not sure. It's the easiest way to make sense of the situation right now.

"I just came to get my belongings. I apologize for interrupting." I turned my glance towards Camille. "Hi, Camille."

"May we talk outside, please?" Camille asked. I've wanted to see Camille, but never thought it would be in this setting. I could have never visualized this scene in my head.

"Camille, you're naked. I don't think that walking outside would be a good idea." I burst out laughing. They're not laughing. I guess I'm the only one with the decency to attempt to remove some of the obvious tension in the room. I opened the front door and walked outside. The air feels different now. I wish I could describe my emotions at this moment. It's like I'm burning inside with anger in the calmest way. It's hard to explain.

"Marcus, what are you doing here?" Camille is now fully clothed.

"Camille, you do know this is my home, right? I should be asking you that question. There's a lot of questions I should be asking you. Where do you want me to start?" She looked away. "No, don't look away now. You've been having a lot of courage lately. It's time to answer for it now."

"We can't do this here. Tiffany may be listening from the other side of the door."

"Who gives a fuck? My relationship is over. My marriage is over before it even happened, all thanks to you. You didn't get what you want so you had to ruin it for everyone. I applaud you for your work."

"Marcus, you have to understand. This wasn't my intention. I only...."

"This wasn't your intention? Camille, you don't even like women! That was the entire point of you turning into a woman!"

"Lower your voice!" Camille whispered.

"NO, fuck lowering my voice." I took a deep breath. I've always imagined losing my mind, but never knew how or when it would happen. I didn't lose it when my mom died, though I was very close.

"You can't tell Tiffany about my secret. I never told her about our secret." My head is about to explode. I'm convinced that some people really don't listen to themselves speak. I don't have all the sense in the world, but like to think my common-sense levels are pretty high.

"Camille, have you processed the thought that you've ruined my marriage and life from all angles? How do you go from leaving me because of my feelings for another person, to catching feelings for the same person you left me over? How? Please, explain this to me. Please explain how you now have feelings for a woman."

"The heart wants what it wants. I don't think the heart can be controlled. And you're going to stop blaming me for everything. Maybe YOU ruined your life. Maybe YOU ruined your future marriage. I'm the innocent bystander that's found myself caught in the middle. Marcus, I still love you."

"Says the woman who was just in MY home, licking MY fiancé's vagina on MY couch." I burst out laughing. "You have a unique way of loving someone."

"Marcus, there's nothing funny about this situation."

"Everything about this situation is funny. Life in general is funny. Look at life as one big joke to save you from crying. Laughing is a stronger medicine than crying."

"Marcus, why didn't you tell me your mom died? She's been dead. How come I had to find out from Tiffany? What happened to me being that person you could confide in?" I walked away. I'm going to get in my car and leave. I don't care about my belongings. She's asking me about my personal life like we still have some type of friendship or relationship. What in her brain told her that would be a good thing to do?

Here I go again, driving with no destination. I've never felt so alone in my entire life. This is what it feels like to have no one to run to. I really want to go dig up my mom's grave and lay inside the casket with her. I'd lie in the casket until I died from no food or water. The things I would give up just to hear her voice one more time. I sometimes wonder if her death was my karma. Let me not get into that mode of thinking.

Tiffany is calling me. I pressed the decline button. What is she calling me for? Tiffany has taught me to never be sure of anything. I've always been sure of the fact that Tiffany doesn't have a disloyal bone in her body. I've maybe even taken that assumption for granted. Not giving myself a pass, but I've been emotionally damaged for a long time. Screwing up in the relationship was probably inevitable on my part. I didn't think it was in Tiffany's genetic make-up. I'm over it and accept it. Fuck everyone, I only have me in the end.

Chapter 11

The past two weeks have been interesting. I quit my job again, but for good this time. I have found a new job. It's basically the same job at a different building. I want to start somewhere fresh, somewhere I can be alone, a place where no one I know can find me. I like the people. They seem friendlier than the people at my previous job.

I've been sleeping in my car, officially living the homeless life. It isn't as bad as I imagined it to be. I have a gym membership I rarely used because I liked working out at home. The membership has come in handy because I go there to take my showers. All I have to do is act like I'm lifting weights for thirty minutes. I don't come off as suspicious to anyone.

I haven't talked to anyone in my past life. I've even avoided Christina. I know this is selfish of me; I'm just at a point in life where I don't care. Where has caring got me? Everything I've cared about has seemed to come apart. I've convinced myself that caring is everyone's downfall in the end. Stop caring for people and focus on yourself. That's my daily morning lesson to myself.

I want to find an apartment, but feel like that will make it easier for me to be found. I've seriously considered purchasing a sleeping bag and living outside. I don't care if anyone I've known in the past from school sees me. I'm at the point in life where nothing really matters anymore. I've had to experience a few situations to get to this point. Just because we choose to prioritize things doesn't mean it actually matters when you look at the big picture.

As I lay in the backseat of my car, it's hard not to think about what my life should have been. For God's sake, I'm sleeping in a car! I'm supposed to be getting married. How did I go from that to this? Why didn't I see this coming? I've tried looking at my current situation from all angles. I've even tried to remove my narcissistic thinking from the equation. Out of all the answers to come to my mind, I'm not sure which answer is correct.

The non-narcissistic side of me says it's all my fault. I did this to myself. I could have stayed on the right path. I could have not followed the curiosity. I could have not started drinking at an early age. I could have denied my mom's offer for the "Kool-Aid" if I really wanted to. Everything ultimately comes down to a choice, and I made all the wrong choices. Luckily, the non-narcissistic side is wrong. Someone is knocking on my window.

"Marcus!" Great, I know that voice. It's Christina, as always. How did she find me? I'm sleeping in a parking spot at some random apartments. I chose a place I thought no one would look. Well, it looks like I'm wrong. I've been on a hot streak of making the wrong decisions. "Marcus, open the door! I know this is your car! These newer version cars can be tracked."

"Go away!" I hollered from inside of the car. If I wasn't in the backseat I'd crank up the car and leave. If I wanted to be found I would have easily made myself available. She just tried to open the door like it's not one o'clock in the morning. I guess this means she's not going anywhere any time soon.

"Marcus!" She's being loud. I should have been asleep; maybe I wouldn't have heard the ruckus. I got up and opened the door. "What in the fuck is going on?" she asked as she sat down beside me. She closed the door. I'm now annoyed. I have to be up in a few hours to get ready for work.

"Thanks for ruining my sleep," I said in an annoyed tone. "People have to work in the morning. We're all not able to attend work whenever we feel like it and have no worries of getting fired. We're all not in a position to be blessed like you." She punched me in the arm. "Ouch."

"Marcus, you're sleeping in a car! What is going on?" I sighed and shook my head. "Don't shake your head at me! You haven't spoken to me in two weeks. I was on the verge of overdosing on antidepressants. You have to be available when I need someone to talk to. Bryan was screaming at me. Julie was advising me to tell Bryan to fuck off and spend all my time with her."

"If you're still having that problem down there," I pointed to her vagina, "Here's the time to get things done." She punched me in the arm. "Ouch! Christina, you're going to stop hitting me. I'm going to press charges. I've been to jail before. It's not a pretty place."

"When in the hell were you in jail? You never tell me anything!" I now have a headache. I shouldn't have opened the door. I could be sleep right now.

"It's a long story." I took a deep breath.

"All we have is time. We're sitting in the backseat of your car, at one in the morning like I'm some type of prostitute. Why are you sleeping in a car? Why have you been avoiding me?"

"Why are you taking antidepressants?" I asked.

"Because I'm damaged emotionally, mentally, physically, spiritually? Because I'm fucked up? What type of question is that? Because I'm depressed, layer on top of layer? Shit, I can go on for hours. We're not talking about me! What's going on with you?"

"Are you sleeping in here with me? We can always talk about this in the morning. I'm actually tired and tired of my thoughts keeping me up. We can sleep in the car together and bond like we used to when we were kids. We can relive old moments." Christina shook her head. "Why are you shaking your head?"

"Marcus, you're sleeping in a car! We are not reliving any moments! This reminds me of living in a shelter home when I was too stubborn to come back to Florida to move in with my parents. That wasn't a happy part of my life! What are we doing here? You're avoiding my question. You could have slept in my house. What is going on in that brain of yours?"

"You don't want to know these thoughts in my head," I truthfully replied. "These thoughts may scare you. I'm a narcissist, remember? I'm starting over in my car. This is all about me and my attempt at getting my life reorganized. I've blocked EVERYONE out and decided to focus on me. Everything that happens, I find a way to revolve it around me, so that's what I'm doing. I'm being in narcissistic mode."

"Fuck you, Marcus. You want everything to be about you? Fine, everything will be about you. We are going to sleep in this car. You're not going to work tomorrow. We are going to figure this out. You're out here living in a car because you want to start over? Who does this type of shit?" I closed my eyes. How wonderful, I'm already about to miss a day of work from a job I just started, and I'm sharing my bed with someone I wish wasn't here. What a wonderful night.

I opened my eyes. I have a headache from my head basically being on the window for hours. "Christina, you scared me," I said as I turned my glance to my left. Christina looks the exact same way as she did before I fell asleep. She's staring at the driver's seat like she's in a trance. "Christina, did you sleep at all?"

"I surely did not," she replied. "I've been looking at this same spot for hours. I'm an insomniac, sleep rarely comes my way. I can easily go forty-eight hours without any sleep, maybe seventy-two hours if I tried. My thoughts come alive at night. I didn't realize you'd fallen asleep. I guess I'd zoned out. Did you sleep good? Are you ready to talk to me? How do you shower?"

"I have a job I just started. I can't miss any days so soon. I haven't even been there a month yet." The few clothes and shoes I've purchased are in the trunk. I haven't attempted to go get my belongings from Tiffany. She should also give me that engagement ring back. Now my cycle of thoughts are about to be about her.

"Marcus, that's not my problem. You need help. Leaving you to figure things out on your own doesn't seem to be serving you well. We all need a shoulder to lean on sometimes. From the look of things, you've decided to avoid every shoulder that may be available to you. Hold on, where is Tiffany?" I closed my eyes.

"You ever want to say the truth but realize how horrible it'll sound once the words come out your mouth?" I opened my eyes.

"No, because I realized a long time ago that the truth is ugly and so is this world. The only reason this world seems beautiful is because of all the lies. It may be because of our addiction to instant gratification. We always want to be happy. I think people in general are aware of that so they lie with good intentions. If I lie to you with a good conscience, is that considered bad? Let's say I'm lying to you to avoid making you unhappy about something you have no control over."

"Isn't it still considered a lie?" I asked. She shrugged her shoulders. I understand her point of view. It's almost like the world was created backwards. I want to tell her my situation just to receive feedback. I feel like I'd be too vulnerable if I was to do that, and I hate…. damn, I really am a narcissist. I can't give up control even if it may benefit me. Maybe it won't benefit me, then I'll be powerless.

"Did your attempt to work things out fail?" I nodded my head. "Holy shit, are you serious? Did she catch you cheating like I hoped she would? Did you use the excuse of her being gay to cover the real story?" I shook my head. It's amazing that my actions didn't break us up. The one thing I feared daily turned out to be irrelevant. I could say that cheating is the reason Camille is in our lives, but I was expecting to get caught. I visualized a million different ways I'd get caught, and tried to think of a million lies to match each scenario. In the end, none of it mattered.

"I'm never going to admit to cheating. That woman was just a friend. I'll never understand why she was in your dream though I wondered for a while. Things just went left with Tiffany. Shit happens in relationships that you can't control." Christina shook her head.

"You want me to tell you how I know you're lying? You only curse around me when you're lying. Yes, it's been a habit of yours since we were kids. Now, how about you tell me the truth. What's the real reason you two ended the relationship?" I hate that Christina knows me so well. It really bothers me. It almost makes me feel like we're connected forever because she knows me better than anyone else, though I will never admit it to her. The only other person to know me so well is now dead. I kind of feel like I am telling the truth. I honestly don't know what I'm feeling. I'm a walking ball of confusion.

"I have to get to work. May we talk about this later?" She squinted her eyes at me. I guess that means I'm not going to work. I really want to go get a bottle of liquor. Maybe Christina and I can drink and talk. Maybe I'll pour my feelings out with liquor in my system. I'll probably say more than I intend to and regret it later. I used to say liquor had no effect on me anymore. That was just another lie I was telling myself.

"How has your mom dying changed you?" she asked. Where did this question come from? How does she go from asking about my relationship to asking about my mom? She's asking a question I've given no thought to. I really don't know how to answer the question. "If you don't have an answer then forget I asked. I know that question was very random. My mind has a tendency to drift off into weird, random, areas." I wish I was at work. I can't think as much because I'm still getting adjusted to the job's culture and people.

"How has my mom's death changed me? A part of me is dead and will never be alive again. Half of my body is functioning perfectly. The other half is numb. Honestly, I've ignored the numbness and continued trying to live. You've brought it back to my attention. I tell others I've accepted it. The truth is I'll never accept it. I'll never understand God's reasoning behind it. You were actually right about me when you were assuming she was dead and how I'd handle it."

"It's been complete torture for me," Christina admitted. "My trips to Urgent Care and the emergency room have increased to the point that the workers know me when I walk in. They're prescribing me with different pills. I have these horrible dreams with her in them. The pills are supposed to put me to sleep but I hate sleeping!"

"Christina...."

"Then your selfish ass is supposed to be the person I'm able to run to when I'm experiencing all of this craziness. But noooo, not with Marcus. Mr. Narcissist feels like since he's having a minor midlife crisis he can just attempt to disappear from the world." I sighed.

"Well, it is a midlife crisis," I stated. "Getting away before you do something you'll regret is probably the best idea." I'm hungry and haven't eaten a real meal since I've been living in my car. I've been eating a bunch of McDonalds, Burger King, and Popeyes. I can feel the difference on the inside. Even though I have a gym membership, I refuse to exercise hard. Fuck being healthy.

"Once you stop thinking about yourself for two seconds, you'll realize you have a friend that needs you. That friend that's always needed you since being kids, needs you more than ever now because she's going crazy." She opened the door and got out. I can still make it to work on time but rather sit here. Maybe I should find a liquor store.

****

It's been six weeks and I'm still living in my car. It has shown me I can really live with less. Things I thought I needed are really things I enjoyed having. I still haven't had a real meal and have about twelve pounds of fat on my stomach to show for it. I'll eventually get in the gym and lose it. I used to pride myself on having a nice body. The pride hasn't been there lately.

Ego won't let me better my situation. I know I don't have to sleep here anymore. I've saved all my checks from work. I have enough to start living a decent life. I could be living with Christina. She's been having seizures all of a sudden and would like me to be there. Why would I decline that offer? I don't feel worthy of being needed, even on a friend level. I'll end up doing something to let her down also. I rather save us the disappointment.

I got out the car. It's been a while since I've visited Mom's grave. I brought a bottle of Hennessy this time. Maybe I'll hear her voice better with liquor in my system. Hold on, it's someone standing in front of my mom's grave. Wow, it's Tiffany. A bunch of different emotions just rushed through my body. I should turn around and get back into my car.

"What are you doing here?" I asked as I reached her. She quickly turned around. I feel like I haven't seen her in years. She's still wearing the engagement ring. I can't read what her eyes are saying. I think it was her that told me the eyes never lie. She looks the same but has seemed to lose the glow she used to have.

"Sometimes, when I want to get away, I come here. This is the last place anyone would expect me to be. It's the loneliest place you can be, around a bunch of dead people." She looked down at my bottle of Hennessy. "What, are you some type of alcoholic now?" I laughed and shook my head.

"This was Mom's favorite liquor. I just wanted to spend some time with her and figured what better way than with a bottle of her favorite liquor." She grabbed the bottle away from me.

"OK, now we will spend time with her." She opened the bottle and took two swallows. The grimace on her face says it all. "Marcus, what is this? It tastes like death." I laughed and grabbed the bottle back. "How could your mom love something that tastes so horrible?"

"Is this your first time having liquor?" I asked. She nodded her head. "This wouldn't have been my first choice for a beginner." I sat down by Mom's tombstone. "My mom loved it, and since it was her love, it is now my love whenever I decide to have a cup of liquor." I still can't seem to stop lying to Tiffany. We're not even together anymore. She sat down by me.

"What do you think she would say if she was alive and looking at how things have turned out?" She grabbed the bottle from me. Well, this wasn't a conversation I was expecting to have today. It's hard to answer her question because of all the lies I've buried underneath the surface. Can I finally be open with her, now that we're not together? Of course not.

"I think she would be as confused as I am about the entire situation." She took a swallow from the bottle. "She would probably wonder how we got to this point. She was the only person who knew I was proposing to you. I'm pretty sure it would be mindboggling to her. She would be sad, probably reliving a situation she experienced. In that sense, it's probably better she's dead."

"I've come here a few times." I reached to grab the bottle from her. She slapped my hand away. "I still can't believe she's not here. Marcus, what happened? How did our lives do a 180?"

"How are you and Camille? How are you enjoying being in a new relationship? Have the two of you figured out the new date for your wedding?" I burst out laughing. Maybe it's because the liquor is in my system, but this conversation doesn't hurt as much as I expected it to.

"Camille and I are in an interesting place, and I'm not sure if it's a good or bad thing. Being in a new relationship has been different. I'm still adjusting to it. It sometimes feels like Camille used to be a man before. Her levels of understanding are amazing. The way she caresses me is a unique experience. I'm not in love, but am experiencing feelings I never knew were possible to feel. I'm vibrating on a higher frequency. This may all seem like a good thing, but not when I was content with how the old situation was." She took two more swallows. Tiffany and I are really sharing a bottle of liquor. This would have never happened while we were together.

"Well, I'm happy to know that you're happy and I wish the two of you the best." I looked at the sky. I wonder is Mom looking down on us right now. I took the bottle of liquor.

"I never said I was happy, Marcus."

"You never said you we're unhappy, Tiffany." She looked up at the sky. "I've come to the conclusion that not accepting things will not change the outcome. I'm tired of spending hours trying to figure out how things went wrong. You eventually realize that everything isn't meant to be understood. If it was possible to understand everything that would make you God." She took the bottle from me. The bottle is almost empty. We went through that quickly.

"She told me to come back to you." She took a big swallow and put the bottle down. I think my heart just stopped. "I know that's mindboggling to hear, but she really did suggest it." *God, take me away now.*

"What was your response?" I asked. I honestly don't know why I asked her that. I don't want to know the answer. I need another bottle of Hennessy ASAP. I shouldn't have come here today. Why didn't I choose to come tomorrow?

"I told her no," she replied. I think my heart just stopped again. I feel myself getting light-headed. I will be fine. I believe I heard her wrong.

"What?"

"I told her no," she repeated. "I thought it was a horrible suggestion. How are you going to come into my life, persuade me to leave my fiancé, change my life forever on a sexual and mental level, then suggest I go back to my fiancé? Let's not forget that she's a woman!"

"I really don't know what to say." I'm now mad that I shared the bottle of liquor with her. That entire bottle could have left me sleep right next to my mom's tombstone. That was the plan. There's an awkward silence in the air. It's the silence that's implying we both want to say something but don't know how to say it.

"She said we should have taken more time to think about you in the process. Yes, the connection between her and I is very strong. Yes, what we have may be something special, but what about you? What have you done to deserve this? That was her question to me and I had no answer. It was a very interesting conversation, to say the least."

"I have a headache. I need to go to the liquor store to get another bottle. Being in deep thought wasn't in my plans today." I stood up. I'm slightly drunk but the liquor store is nearby.

"Marcus, she's leaving me. Please, sit back down. I need clarity on the situation." My heart wants me to sit back down and help her figure this out. My mind is reminding me that I should walk away. This situation has nothing to do with me. The truth is telling me otherwise. This has everything to do with me. I'm just using my mind to lie to myself.

"I don't know what you want me to say." I'm not sitting back down. I was free from this situation. I'd accepted the fact I'd lost my fiancé. It seems like every time I accept something, it gets thrown back in my face. Great, it's now started to rain. Florida has the weirdest weather. It goes from sunny weather to rain in an instant. Tiffany stood up.

"May we go to your place and continue this conversation?" I smiled and shook my head.

"My car is my place of residence. It's a long story. I'm going to find me an apartment soon. I just wanted to try an alternate way of living life, to make a long story short." She has a confused look on her face, which is understandable.

"How about you come back to my place and update me on what's been going on with your life. You've obviously made some changes. I can't believe you're sleeping in a car." She shook her head and walked away. My way of living didn't seem so outrageous until I mentioned it to her. My day is going nothing like how I had it planned.

"I'm not trying to upset Camille. You said she's leaving you. That doesn't mean she's left you yet." The last person I want to see right now is Camille.

"Camille is at work. I'll text her and tell her you're coming over if that makes you feel better. I'm sure she wouldn't mind. You're the reason we know each other." She continued walking. It seems like I'm the reason for everything.

"I'm coming." I feel her legs shaking. I grabbed her waist. "I…..I," She closed her eyes tightly. I feel it all coming out. What am I doing here? What in the hell just happened? She leaned onto me.

"Marcus, what just happened?" She got off me and laid on the pillow beside me. She's actually asking a very good question. I will blame the bottle of liquor I picked up on the way here. It had to be the liquor. God is my witness when I say I had no plans of having sex with Tiffany.

"I think we had a little too much to drink," I replied. We're in 'our' room that no longer looks or feels like our room. It has been redesigned. The bed is the same. This is my bed. This bed has now had Tiffany vs I, Camille vs I, and Camille vs Tiffany on it. How did my life get to this point?

"What is my life turning into?" Tiffany asked. "I'm officially a cheater. I've become what I promised myself I wouldn't." Tiffany's phone just vibrated. I hope that isn't Camille calling. My luck can't be this bad. "Wow, Camille just said that she's been thinking a lot, and maybe us separating isn't the best decision. No, life isn't supposed to happen like this. This sounds like something that happens in a movie."

"Maybe I should go." I got out the bed. "You probably should wash your sheets. I would throw them away, but that may look too suspicious." I put on my boxers and shorts.

"Marcus, we just had sex. Your energy is back onto me. How do I move forward with life? At least when Camille and I had sex I'd removed myself away from you. Camille has a high sex drive. She will more than likely want to have sex tonight. How do I go about having sex with her? There's too much guilt on my body." I took a deep breath.

"Who has the better sex?" I asked. "It doesn't matter, I'm just curious."

"Her sex is better." It feels like a sharp knife just went through my heart. I'm not showing it, but that hurts. How is this even possible? I also believe Camille's sex is better than Tiffany's, and no, that's not because my ego is bruised. "What made you ask me that?"

"Tell her your period has arrived." Yes, I'm intentionally ignoring her question. "This is a unique situation for you because you're not a liar. I'm not sure how you're going to hold up trying to lie to Camille while she's directly in your face." Sadness is on Tiffany's face.

"Marcus, I never lied to you once during our relationship. This is all new to me. I no longer know myself. I feel like I'm a totally different person now, and the change happened quickly. I'm more of an emotional person. It may be because I'm dealing with an unknown situation now. With you, every day wasn't perfect, but I knew what I had, and I know what I had was real. Now, life seems like a fairytale. I'm experiencing remarkable highs and lows. It's all becoming overwhelming."

"You will figure it out, you always do." I put on my shirt. "You're a deep thinker. That's the trait I loved about you the most. You're good at problem solving. You will figure everything out."

"Marcus, I'm not sure if I know that Tiffany anymore. Curiosity has ruined my life. I should have stayed in my box. When Camille attempted to kiss me, I should have quickly pushed her away before our lips connected. I've ruined my life. I'm the one to blame for all this. I ruined you, I ruined us, I've ruined everything." I took another deep breath.

"The great thing about life is that if you're blessed to see another day, you have another twenty-four hours to make your life right again." I walked out the room. I'm now looking around the living room. Everything has been changed. Any signs of Marcus have been removed. My life was slightly better before coming back here, which I promised myself I never would. The old feelings are returning.

I cranked up the car. I'm probably thinking too much, which I tend to do a lot, but life doesn't seem real sometimes. I hate when too many thoughts start going through my head at once. This would be a good time to go see my therapist, but since I'm still being stubborn with him, I'll talk to my other therapist. I now keep my diary inside of my glove compartment.

Dear Diary,

I haven't spoken to you in a while. I've tried figuring it out in my head, which has done nothing but cause major headaches. I now sit in front of my old home, where I just had sex with my ex fiancé, who was taken away from me by the person I planned on leaving her for. Welcome to the life of Marcus. Tiffany isn't over me yet. She made love to me like she misses me. The passion levels were too high for it to be considered as casual sex. Though I was slightly drunk, I could feel every moment. At this present moment, my emotion is that I miss her. I miss her more than anything else in the world right now. Will this emotion change? Quite possibly, but it's what I'm feeling right now. No, Camille's knocking on my passenger's window. We will resume this conversation later.

Marcus

"What are you writing?" she asked as she closed the door. No one told her to get in. My heart is beating fast. Why am I so nervous? Maybe because I have Tiffany's scent on me. Wait, why should I care? This girl is the reason for all the dysfunction in my life.

"What do you want?" I meanly asked. Camille is looking beautiful. Unfortunately, there's a lot of ugliness beneath the beauty.

"Marcus, I'm confused about everything right now. This thing Tiffany and I have is eating me up on the inside. I have a tough time sleeping at night. This isn't how I planned for my life to turn out." I shook my head. There's sincerity in her voice but I don't believe it. I'm done being the idiot in this whole ordeal.

"Did you come to this realization before or after you put your mouth and tongue on my fiancé's vagina?" Camille looked away. "Looking away isn't going to answer the question, Camille. You're the one that stepped into my car. You obviously wanted to talk."

"OK, Marcus, I fucked up. Is that what you want to hear? Will that satisfy your ego? My intentions were never bad, but bad has come out of my intentions." She took a deep breath. "I love you and Tiffany with the same amount of love." I looked away, not because I'm avoiding the conversation, but I'm refraining myself from saying something I may regret.

"Whatever you say, Camille." If this was my home like it used to be, I'd get out and leave right now. I want to tell her she's crazy and I regret ever meeting her, but know that would be considered mean and rude. I also want to tell her I really miss her, but that would make me sound crazy. Maybe we're all crazy. I need a drink. "You should go spend time with your girlfriend."

"Marcus, do you believe me when I say I never intended for this to happen? I never intended to break up your relationship. I just wanted all your love, and left when I realized I wasn't going to get it."

"But somehow, someway, you end up in Florida again. Not only did you end my relationship, but also convinced my fiancé to fall in love with you. You're a smooth criminal. I think you had this planned for a long time. I think this plan goes back months in advance. You had some lucky breaks, like me getting into that car accident. It gave you your silent way in."

"Marcus...." I put my hand up.

"I'm not done. I think you're a person that thrives off manipulating people. It makes you feel powerful. This messy situation makes you feel powerful. You've created one big love triangle! I hope you're getting off on what you've created. You're doing a great job with ruining lives!"

"Fuck you, Marcus!"

"Too late! You've already screwed up my life from every angle, and did it purposely." She quickly hopped on top of me and started to kiss me. What is going on right now? We're directly in front of where she lives. *Marcus, stop thinking!* No, I will not stop thinking. She's trying to control the situation! I feel myself getting erect. She quickly put her hands inside my shorts and started rubbing my dick. I pushed her off me. I'm breathing very hard.

"If anyone is confused about all of this, it's me. Remember that when you decide to form more horrible ideas in your head about me and my intentions. However this turns out, please let this be the last time I see you." She opened the door. "I wish you the best, Marcus." She got out and slammed the door. The love triangle continues.

I'm headed to the liquor store. I'm going back to my original plan, which was to buy me a bottle and sit by my mom and talk to her. The store clerk is going to be confused after seeing me for a third time in less than twenty-four hours. I don't blame him if he judges me. I probably deserve all the judgment. If he had any idea on how crazy my life has become, he'd probably advise me to buy more liquor.

Chapter 12

"Sir, you have to get up." I opened my eyes. Wow, I fell asleep by my mom's tombstone. "Don't worry," the man continued, "I won't alert anyone about the empty bottles of liquor. I have a feeling the person under this tombstone is someone very special to you." He walked away. He must be the cemetery's caretaker. I have a headache. I went through two and a half bottles of liquor. Why haven't I died yet? What's the plan for my life if there's one?

I have four missed calls. It may be a good thing I left my phone in the car. I don't remember anything after going to the liquor store. I have no clue what I would have said if I would have answered my phone. Christina called me once, my dad called me three times. What does he want? I need to let him know the wedding has been cancelled. No, that's a bad idea. All that's going to do is present the opportunity to ask a bunch of questions I'd like to avoid.

What day is it? Do I have to work today? I feel like I haven't been to work in a long time. I was back on track. It all started to unwind once Christina found me. I was slowly climbing my way out of this hole of sadness. Speaking of the devil, Christina is calling me again. "Yes, Christina," I answered.

"Come visit me in the psych ward," she bluntly stated. She's not even asking me, she's telling me.

"Christina, hell no. I'm not coming to that place. I will admit I'm scared. You can call me a pussy or any other negative word. This time only I will accept it. Why do you keep going there?"

"This place protects me from myself, since my friend would rather live inside of his car than live in a warm home with me, with a comfortable bed, a bathroom, a kitchen, Wi-Fi."

"OK Christina, I get it."

"No, I don't think you do. I had another seizure last night. If you would have been there, you could have helped me, but nooo, you rather be selfish. You probably weren't doing anything important. I'd bet a million dollars you were somewhere drunk.

You probably didn't hear the phone." How does she know me so well? "You're going to kill yourself with all that liquor. I'm shocked you still have a liver."

"Christina, does it give you some type of satisfaction with trying to make me feel bad? You do a great job in trying. Why do you have to be so negative towards my life decisions?"

"Well, excuse the hell out of me for trying to care about your well-being. Excuse me for already living the life you're currently trying to live. Don't you realize how fucked I am? It all started with liquor. I eventually graduated to other things and look at me now! I get joy out of being in a psych ward!"

"Christina, I'm never going to try drugs."

"I used to say the same thing. I swear, you act like you're so sure about everything. Life has a way of throwing you curveballs, unless you're a special case. I thought life was going to be great for me. Now I live with a bunch of voices in my head. It seems like every negative psychological term has my name associated with it. We're getting off topic. Stop being a pussy and come visit me at the psych ward. I need you. Does that ego of yours hear me? I said I need you."

"I'm only coming there to get you out. I don't like you being there. You know what? I'll move in with you. I'll do anything to keep you out of there. You being in there makes my nerves bad. I know I have a horrible way of showing it, but I really do care about you. You being in there gives me…..it makes me feel weak, with a lack of control." The call ended. I know what that means. I somehow found a way to make that conversation about me. At least I agreed to move in with her.

****

Dear Diary,

I've been living with Christina for three weeks and it's been the most interesting experience ever. Things are worse than she led me to believe. There's no way she should be living alone. It's to the point that I'm scared to sleep, with the fear that something may happen to her. She wakes up screaming in the middle of the night. I'll run into her room and ask her what's wrong, she'll tell me Julie has been bothering her. I tried to sleep with her for a few days. That was a horrible experience. She wakes up with cold sweats. She's had two seizures since I've been here. I may not show it but I'm scared for her. I'm scared I'm going to lose her. I've already lost my mom. I couldn't imagine what would happen if I lost Christina. She still won't tell me what started her on this unique path, but I blame me. I should have been there. What type of friend am I? What could I've been doing that was more important than being around my best friend to protect her? I don't have to know what happened, it's clear that it was bad. I blame me.

Marcus

Tiffany is calling me. I haven't spoken to her in three weeks. We have nothing to talk about. I don't care if her and Camille finally separated. I don't care if they're deciding to get married. Just leave me out of it. "Hello," I answered in an annoyed tone. I really have better things to have my mind on than Tiffany. We all should admit we're confused and go our separate ways.

"Marcus, I'm pregnant." My heart just stopped. There's no emotion in her voice. "Before you get to wondering how, just know that I stopped getting the depo shot a while ago. Us getting married had me thinking about kids. I didn't see the point in getting it while messing with a woman. Marcus, our child is in my stomach."

"Shit," I said. I think I need a nap. I don't know what to say. What is going on right now? How do I have a child on the way? I know my inner self is going to tell me to breathe. Breathing isn't going to help me figure things out. I feel a panic attack coming. I need water.

"Marcus, what are we going to do? How am I going to tell Camille? We seem to be rekindling things. How has my life become one cycle of confusion? It seems like it happened overnight. My parents don't know about Camille but know we've separated. How do I explain this to anyone? I have a life in my stomach." My mind is not sorting things out quickly enough.

"I'm going to go to the liquor store and try to figure things out."

"Marcus, you sound like an alcoholic." I almost said something I'm sure I would have regretted later. I almost admitted to being an alcoholic. I just realized I'm exposing alcoholic tendencies. I'm losing control over everything, my life included.

"FUCK YOU," Christina screamed from the other room. "No, get away from me. I hate you! Bryan, get her away. Bryan, listen to me! Well, fuck you too. Joe, rescue me! No, Julie, I'm not coming with you. I have Marcus, my hero. He will beat you up. Fuck all of you. MARCUS, HELP ME!" She's now crying. I want to cry right now. I can't help Christina. I can't even help myself. I'm feeling like a complete failure.

"Marcus, are you there?" I didn't realize I'm still holding the phone. What am I supposed to do? Though it was the wrong scenario, I loved feeling Camille on top of me. All the feelings instantly rushed back over me. I believe I'm at the point where I've accepted her being a transgender if it's true. My love hasn't changed. I've constantly tried to fight it but the feeling is still there. I still hold an inkling of hope that it's not true.

"Well, Tiffany, I guess we should get prepared to have a baby."

"Marcus, we're not together. I'm in a confused relationship with a woman. My feelings for her are real. We've had more disagreements than our entire relationship but something won't let me leave. She's attempted to walk away multiple times. She always ends up staying. Something strong is trying to break us apart. Something stronger is keeping us together." I took a deep breath.

"Well, I don't believe in abortions so we need to figure something out." I refuse to send my child where my mom is because I'm having life complications. I want to have this child, though I can't imagine me being a dad. I don't know how to be a dad. My dad is the last example I want to follow.

"So, I guess I should tell Camille the news." I ended the call. She knows what she must do. I know a bunch of unnecessary questions were about to come next. No, I don't know how she should tell Camille. No, I don't know what's going to happen after she tells Camille. No, I don't know what this means for us. I don't know anything and hate that I don't have any answers. Crying about it won't solve anything. I need to figure things out but don't know how.

****

Four days have passed and I haven't heard from Tiffany. I have the urge to call her but won't allow myself to. I've convinced myself that calling her won't help anything. She's still trying to figure things out. A year ago, no one could have convinced me my life would be at this point. For the past three days I've been drinking vodka, hoping it would push away the thoughts. If anything, it's enhanced my thoughts on the exact thing I'm trying to forget about.

Someone is knocking on the door. It has to be Tiffany. Christina is at work and no one else knows I live here. I always planned on Christina living with me. How did the opposite happen? I probably should stop planning things in life. Life never goes as planned. I opened the door. Great, it's Camille, and she doesn't look happy. I closed the door as she walked in.

"So, this is how you punish me for feeling like I punished you? You purposely impregnate Tiffany when you know she doesn't believe in abortions?" She quickly slapped me. "Is this how you do things? Is this how you hurt people you care about?"

"I didn't purposely impregnate Tiffany," I calmly stated. She slapped me again.

"BULLSHIT."

"Camille, if you slap me again I'm calling the police. I'm not going to jail over a quick reflex on my part. I know you're upset, but you're going to talk to me like a civilized human being." The anger on her expression hasn't left. She looks like she wants to slap me again. I pointed to the couch. "Would you like to sit down?"

"No, I rather stand," she meanly replied. She's balled up her fists. It may be smart to call the cops right now. I don't have time to have any misdemeanors or felonies on my record. "So, would you like to explain yourself?"

"What am I explaining? Tiffany and I had unprotected sex like we've been doing. You can't forget that this woman was my fiancé before you came into the picture. Why am I doing the explaining? You should be doing the explaining."

"Marcus," she started slowly, "I love her."

"I love her too! What is that supposed to mean?"

"Marcus, I love you also." I swear, she makes me want to scream. They say to never have regrets. Well, at this moment I regret everything. My entire life now seems like a life of mistakes. I can clearly see each mistake I've made in the past year. Why couldn't someone tell me each decision would lead me to this exact moment? "Marcus, how did life become so confusing?" I put my hands over my face. This is too much stress to handle at once.

"My life didn't become stressful until I allowed you into it. I'm blaming me more than I'm blaming you. If you really cared about either of us you'd walk away." Camille shook her head.

"Is that your great solution? You think me walking away is going to solve everything?" I nodded my head. "Marcus, I think you've fallen in love with the cycle of unhappiness. I've tried leaving, you've tried leaving. Why can't you realize attempting to leave doesn't solve anything? It almost seems like it's fate for us to be together."

"Are you referring to me or Tiffany?" I asked. "And how come no one will explain to me exactly how you made your way back to Florida? You had moved to California." Camille took a deep breath.

"I'm the strength to each of your weaknesses. What Tiffany lacks, I'm able to fulfill for you. What you lack, I'm able to fulfill for Tiffany. I'm the big missing piece to the puzzle. When I walk away, one of you, if not both will always call me back into your life. I'll decline the offer but will be persuaded that I am needed. Who doesn't like feeling wanted and needed? So, am I the problem? Or is it the two of you?" I now have a headache.

"I need a drink." I walked towards the couch and sat down. It's scary, but she's right. What's scarier is that Tiffany is now under the same trance. Some type of way we've all become reliant on each other. "I'm going to tell her." Camille sat by me. "I'm going to tell her everything. I'm going to even mention the transgender part." Camille placed her hand on my thigh.

"Marcus, we've come too far. At this point why would any of that matter? What's going to be the outcome? All that's going to happen is Tiffany going through a state of confusion and anger. After she gets over it, and she will, we will be right back at this point in life. Don't delay what's already here. Marcus, we all have feelings for each other. The feelings are genuine." I now feel like I need to be in someone's psych ward.

"I'm not going to be a part of it. I don't want to be in this triangle. I rather suffer in loneliness and fight the urge. I'll walk away now. You two can keep the baby. I'm not going to be a part of this circus. Yes, I know it's all my fault. That's something I'm willing to live and die with." I have a massive headache that only a drink can cure.

"Marcus, denying what the heart wants is unhealthy for the mind and body." She leaned over and kissed me. I lied onto the couch as she got on top of me. Her lips are so soft. I could kiss on them forever. I quickly unbuttoned my pants. Her tongue tastes so good.

"Who in the fuck are you?" We quickly stopped kissing. Shit, it's Christina. I didn't lock the door. If she would have used her key I would have heard it. "Hey, you're the mistress. Are you the reason Marcus and Tiffany broke up?" Christina has a blank expression on her face. There's no anger, sadness, nothing. I hate when she displays this expression because it's hard to know what she's thinking. It's even hard to figure out what she's thinking when she's happy.

"I think you have me confused with someone else," Camille said as she stood up. I've been caught in the act. It's going to be hard to lie my way out of this one. This is the last situation I need in my life right now.

"Please, sit back down," Christina nicely suggested. "I'd like to get to know you." Camille sat back down. This isn't going to go well. Christina turned her glance to me. "So, who do I start questioning first?" She turned her glance back to Camille. "Forgive me for not introducing myself. I'm Christina, I'm clinically diagnosed as psychotic and Marcus is my best friend." This definitely isn't going to go well. "This is my home you're in, the home Marcus has a room in. We sometimes sleep in the same bed. He knows how fucked up in the head I am, to put it nicely."

"Christina," she put her hand up, motioning for me to hush. Camille has fear in her eyes. I don't know why she has fear in her eyes but I don't blame her. She doesn't know how crazy Christina is. Now that I think about it, I don't know how crazy Christina is. This could get ugly.

"So, you're the reason for everything?" Christina asked Camille. "You're the reason he's living here? You're the reason he's been so unhappy, but has been trying hard to hide it? You're the reason his mom died?"

"That reminds me, you never explained to me how your mom died," Camille stated. Great, here goes a road I don't feel like going down. "Why didn't you tell me she was dead when it happened? Was that the reason for your random acts of disappearing?" I want to scream and run out of this house. I've never screamed before. I wonder what my screams sound like. "Marcus, you never tell me anything!"

"Well, welcome to The Marcus Show," Christina sarcastically stated. "The show of mystery and secrets. The show where you feel so much of him but realize you know nothing at all. By the kissing I assume the two of you have had sex. Wow, you women are stupid." She shook her head. "So, who's going to reveal the news?" My eyes widened.

"What news are you referring to?" I asked.

"Who's going to tell Tiffany you're the reason they're not together?" She pointed at Camille. "I saw you in one of my dreams, then saw you at Marcus' apartment, now I see you at my home. Marcus has been trying to deny you for a while. Well, he can't deny you now. You've ruined his life, which means you've ruined mine because he's my best friend and we're connected."

"Christina, she's a transgender," I calmly stated. Camille's eyes have shifted towards me. I'm looking at Christina but feel her eyes burning into my skull. "I've caught feelings for a transgender and have been confused about it ever since. I've tried to push her away but my soul wouldn't allow me to. My life has been in a whirlwind ever since."

"Marcus, what are you doing?" Camille angrily asked.

"I've never been interested in cheating. I always thought cheating was for the weak. Cheating to me meant you had no willpower and really didn't care about the person you're with. It meant you don't know how to care about a person and in the end everything is all about you. I've always thought cheating was the ultimate act of selfishness. Now, look at me, doing the same thing with someone who was born as a male! I've thrown away my future marriage, my morals, and everything else I considered positive all because of my new addiction." I pointed at Camille.

"So, that's all I am to you?" Camille asked. "I'm just some addiction you're hoping to get over?"

"I've been telling you this the entire time! What are you talking about?"

"I get it," Christina started, "I understand now." We quickly turned our glance towards her. "This has been the plan. This was the escape plan for if something ever goes wrong. You'd use the transgender route for sympathy. Cheating wouldn't seem so harsh with that type of confusion involved. Are you two really that idiotic? Do you think someone is really going to believe that story? Marcus, have you been taking some of my pills that has you having delusional thoughts?"

"Great." I buried my face into my hands. I've finally revealed the truth. I thought I would feel better. I thought it would feel like 100 bricks have been removed from my back. In the end, my truth isn't believable. I want to run away to another country and cry for a full month. When I feel like I'm out of tears, I'd stop for a day and cry some more.

"Marcus, get out. Pack your things and leave your key. You're not the Marcus I used to know. You'd go to extreme lengths to cover your tracks, including lying to your best friend. I guess that means you don't care about me either." I stood up. What is going on right now?

"No, I'm not going anywhere. Christina, you need me here. I'm not leaving you here alone." I took a deep breath. "I need a drink."

"Are you in a love square?" Camille asked.

"A love square?"

"You, me, Tiffany, and now Christina. How can you love us all? I know you can't love us all equally. Are you addicted to punishment? Are you addicted to being hurt?"

"Who said I love Christina?" Christina threw her hands up. "No, that came out wrong. I don't love Christina in that way. Christina is the one woman I'll never have sex with."

"We should have had oral sex," Christina mumbled. "Pussy."

"We are getting off topic," I said. "Camille, go home. I'll talk to you later once I figure things out, if that's even possible." I've just realized my world is surrounded by women. I don't have any male of significance in my life. The only male was my therapist, and I've pushed him away.

"Marcus, leave Tiffany alone. I have her heart now and you obviously can't figure out what you want in life."

"What?" Christina asked.

"Tiffany is carrying my child. I can't leave her alone. Did you think I was serious? I would never leave my child with the two of you!"

"Whoa, wait a minute." Christina chimed in.

"Are you trying to say two women can't raise a child?" Camille asked. "Marcus, are you being a sexist? Okay, now the real Marcus is revealing himself."

"You're not a real woman!" I lashed out. I regret saying that, but it's too late to take it back. Sadness has come across Camille's face. She shook the expression away.

"Well whose mouth did you just have your tongue in, since I'm not a woman? Whose pussy can't you get enough of? Who is the person you can't seem to leave alone? What does all of this say about you?"

"Camille, fuck you!"

"No, Marcus, fuck you! Fuck you for everything!" Camille stood up.

"Are you two really going to keep this narrative going?" Christina asked. She touched Camille's midsection, causing her to jump. "You have a pussy. You're a woman. What in the fuck are you two talking about? I'm already crazy in the head; the two of you aren't making it any better for me."

"Bye Marcus." Camille opened the door and walked out. I put both of my palms on my forehead. What has happened to my life? Piece by piece it's fallen apart. I don't know what I'm doing anymore.

"Marcus, what's going on?" Christina asked with confusion in her voice. I walked away. I'm not trying to be rude, I just don't know how to answer her question.

****

"How did you know you loved him more than you loved my mom?" I asked my dad. We are back at the same Starbucks for the third time. I instructed him not to bring his family. He's probably wondering why I keep bringing him back to Starbucks. Logic would say that our interactions at Starbucks haven't gone great, so it may be a good idea to meet somewhere else. Unfortunately, I haven't been logical about a lot of things lately.

"Son, that's such a tricky question. Why don't we catch up on getting to know each other before we dive into the deep topics? Have you come up with a wedding date yet? I'm really looking forward to it." I'm not going to mention that Tiffany and I are no longer together. I still have a weird hope that the wedding will happen. It's odd how my mind works.

"I don't care about talking about the small things. I don't care to discuss my childhood. You weren't there and I'm over it. My mom raised me the best way she could, even with all the emotional pain you caused. We're past that. Now, answer my question, please." The look in his eyes says he'd walk out if this was our first time meeting. Maybe he's who I get my walking out tendencies from. I blame him for all my bad habits.

"Son, this isn't a conversation I'm comfortable with having." I took a sip from my coffee.

"I would get upset, but I'm realizing so much right now. It's you who I get my narcissistic tendencies from. You really think this conversation is about you like you're the victim. Victim probably isn't the right word, but if there's any victim, it's me. Your actions have caused all the emotional and psychological damage that I may have experienced. This is supposed to be an uncomfortable conversation. We're not friends." Dad took a deep breath.

"Son, have you ever been in an experience you didn't want to explain? The experience was so great that you just wanted to stay living in the moment?" I shook my head in disagreement. I think he knows I'm lying. I want to nod in agreement, but agreeing might insinuate I'm giving him a way out, and that's not the case.

"Nope, I feel like every experience deserves an explanation if needed. The only time this is excluded is in dreams, only because I'm not sure if you can consider a dream an authentic experience." He took a sip from his coffee.

"I never loved him more than I loved your mom." My eyes widened. That's not the answer I was expecting and I can't hide my surprise. "I fell for the act of feeling understood. Well, it isn't an act, it's real. He understood me as a man more than your mom. Most people don't want to be changed; they just want to be understood. Your mom tried to change me, which I don't fault her for because I believe she was trying to change me into a better individual."

"So, essentially you walked away for the easier route?" I asked.

"Hey, I was gay before it was accepted. There was nothing easy about the route I took. I just decided to follow my heart. I think I made the right decision. After I adjusted to the lifestyle I became a happier person."

"So, following your heart meant leaving your son? Your happiness came at the expense of having a damaged son? You're fine with that? You can sleep peacefully at night with your decision? I'm a walking version of you, personality wise. You are who I get all my selfishness from. It doesn't matter how anyone else feels, as long as you're happy. Thanks Marcus, thanks for the horrible genetics." I shook my head.

"Son, no reasoning will satisfy you, and that's understandable. I was young. At that time, you seeing me being around another man in an intimate way just didn't seem like the right situation. I didn't want you to become like me." There's so much to say right now but I will not. His attempt of trying to save me backfired on him in a major way.

"How does your adopted son deal with it?" He took a sip from his coffee. "I take that back, don't answer that question. There's no reason I should have any hate for him. I've told myself this before, but it doesn't change the fact he has what I didn't, because you thought it would be smart to leave me. I hope you never leave him. He doesn't deserve that." My dad looked away. "What's that supposed to mean?"

"Nothing," he quickly replied. "Am I not allowed to look away during our conversation?"

"You're thinking about leaving your significant other and son. I can hear it in your tone. You said you were happy. Why are you thinking about leaving them? You can't do that!" He took a sip from his coffee. "Put the coffee down!" My voice has risen and I don't care.

What's Starbucks going to do? Kick us out? We are paying customers having a friendly debate.

"Lower your voice," he firmly said. "I'm a human being, I make mistakes. I'm allowed to have a change of heart and a change of thoughts. There's no rulebook to this thing we call life. I never said I was leaving them, but has the thought ever crossed my mind? Of course it has. There's nothing wrong with wanting more in life."

"Marcus, you're nothing but an energy vampire. You suck away everyone's energy and move on when you're done, not caring about your victim. It's in your habit loop; you may not be able to control it. It should be against the law for us to have the same name. I'm calling you something different. I want no affiliation with you."

"How can you judge me when you don't even know me?" he asked.

"Because I am you," I meanly replied. "It's like I see myself while talking to you. All your ways and habits you gave me. The difference is I see where it's taken you. I still have time to turn this around before I get stuck in my ways." I stood up. Maybe Starbucks is a bad place to meet up at. My luck just isn't good here.

"Son, please sit down."

"I'm not your son," I said lowly. "You've cursed me, know that you've cursed me, and don't even care. You should have stayed away. Nothing good has come out of you appearing back into my life." People are looking at me. I guess I look odd standing up. I sat back down. Maybe I should calm down. I've been neglecting my breathing techniques, though they've proven to be effective.

"What do you want from me? I'm sorry I'm not this perfect father figure you had pictured in your head. I'm a man full of flaws. Could I have done things differently in the past? Of course I could have. I can't change the past. I can only change the future if you allow me to. I'm still a work in progress just like any other person. I have a lot of horrible ways. I battle my demons daily. I want to be in your life. Things may never be normal, but at least we can have something."

"Fine, we can give it a try. I'm telling you now that I'm a borderline cold-hearted person today. Since my mom, your ex-wife, has been dead I've realized that it's stupid to get close to anyone. You never know when a person is going to die, so why invest in something you don't have any control over? Only to be left with memories when the inevitable happens? I'm tired of memories that are supposed to be happy ones. They end up turning into nightmares because I can't relive the memories."

"I understand," he started, "And I know patience will be important in this relationship. I don't care what happens, I promise I'll never leave you again. You're going to have to push me away this time, and that would be understandable because I can't expect you to forgive me." I nodded my head, stood up, and walked to the entrance. At least this time had a better ending. Tiffany would be proud of me.

I'm now back in the car but don't know my next move. I really have a child on the way. I'm slowly but surely accepting the fact that my heart will never let go of Camille. Tiffany still doesn't know about Camille and me. The right thing to do would be to get Tiffany back and give my child the family structure I never had. That's what I'm going to do.

I pulled up to Tiffany's job and texted her, telling her to come outside. If she doesn't respond, then I'll just have to accept the fact that it's over. What if she keeps my child away from me? I don't think she's that type of person, but can admit that Tiffany isn't the same person. It's like she changed overnight. The once strong-minded woman is now confused and weak. I guess I'm the one to blame for some of her changes.

"What do you want, Marcus?" she asked as she closed the car door. She doesn't look pregnant yet, but her face does look different. It looks like it has added weight. Her cheeks are more bloated.

"I want things to go back to normal. I want us to get back on track. I forgive you for doing whatever you did with Camille. Things could be worse. It could have been with a man." I burst out laughing. She's not laughing. "You have my seed in your stomach. It's made me realize what's important. Us being a family is all that matters to me. My child must have a better family structure than I did. It's not up for debate."

"Marcus, what if I'm happy with Camille? What if what her and I have now feels like a family? I actually thought of telling my parents about her. I know that sounds crazy, you and I both know they won't accept that, but that's how deep my feelings for her are." I feel my head about to explode. "Camille and I have our problems but we seem to always work them out. We're never mad at each other for long." I took a deep breath.

"What about our child?" I asked. "We have to compromise for the kid. This is not about our happiness. This is about our child having the best situation possible. We now have an obligation to give the child the best life possible." Tiffany looked away.

"Why can't we give the child the best life with me staying with Camille?" she asked while looking out the window. I know if I don't start my breathing techniques I'm going to lose my mind.

"Tiffany, I don't want my child looking at Camille as a father figure while I'm in the picture. Excuse me if I'm not comfortable with that scenario. This whole situation has given me constant headaches and I'm usually good at figuring things out. I'm not trying to put this confusion on my child. I know, I know, we could sit down and figure it out. I don't want to figure it out. I want things back to how they were a couple of months ago."

"Everything isn't about what you want, Marcus! Everything can't go your way! The world doesn't revolve around you. That's not how life works. Maybe your plans and God's plans aren't aligned. Have you stopped to give that any thought? Maybe things are supposed to be this way."

"Who are you? What happened to the Tiffany I used to know?"

"She's torn into pieces and is trying to put herself back together. She's not in denial of the fact she doesn't know who she is anymore. She's confused about everything in life and doesn't know what's right and wrong anymore. What's supposed to be right now feels wrong. What's supposed to be wrong now feels right. The Tiffany you knew may be dead and gone."

"You can get out now," I said as I turned to look out the window. Looking at her now hurts. The passenger's door just shut, which means she's gone, maybe forever. Maybe things will forever be changed and I just don't want to accept it. I can't explain how I'm feeling right now on the inside. It's a combination of numbness and sadness. I don't know what to do anymore. What do you do when you've run out of answers?

I've been lying in the dark, crying for hours. This has been my form of meditation for the night. Every thought that comes to my head, I cry to. I've created a mental loop of unhappiness. I know this isn't healthy, but who cares? No one cares about me. Maybe I don't care about me anymore. How did my life become mistake after mistake? Why wasn't I more conscious of this while making the mistakes? Lately, I've heard a lot of people say they have no regrets because those mistakes made them who they are today. My challenge to that is what if you're not happy with the person you've become?

Someone is knocking on my room door. It has to be Christina. She probably finds it odd that my door is closed. I never sleep with my door closed. Did she hear me crying? I'm not getting up to open the door. I just want to lie here and drown in misery. I want to drown in my tears. I have work in the morning but have already made up my mind that I'm not going. They should just fire me.

"Marcus, I know you're sad in there. I heard your cries from my room. I know you're not going to tell me what's wrong, so I'll just sit here by the door until I hear you sleeping peacefully. Don't worry, Marcus, I'm always here for you like you've been there for me, even if you don't want me to be." I can tell she just sat down by the door. It's weird having someone trying to comfort me. I haven't had that in a while, so my first action is to push it away. I'll take care of myself because no one is going to. At the end of the day, all I have is me.

Two hours have passed and I'm still lying here trying to lower my cries. Christina has a great ear, she hasn't left the door yet. I now see what it feels like to be on the other side. She's lucky; I was sitting outside while it was raining. I've heard that crying is the best medicine. Well, I don't feel any better. I'm still hurt and confused on the inside. I still feel alone and blame myself for everything. My journey through life has brought me here. What does it all mean? I'm tired of thinking and crying. I'm going to sleep. Hopefully I wake up with solutions.

"Marcus, are you dead?" I opened my eyes. It must be the next morning. "If you're dead, just know I'm sorry for leaving you all those years ago. I'm sorry I'm not the girl I used to be, and will never be the same again. I've always loved you like a brother. When it seemed like everyone was abandoning me, you've always been there. Through all my being bi-polar, a prescription pills addict, a dysfunctional hormones individual, you've been there for me. I'm not sure if dysfunctional hormones is a real term."

"I'm alive," I hollered from my bed. I guess I should get up now. The truth is I don't want to get up. I rather lie here and be in a slump for the entire day. I've lost all control over my life and am having a hard time accepting it. Every single situation is an unknown now. At least I know if I stayed in my room I'd be safe.

I opened my room door. Yes, Christina is sitting here with a teddy bear. "Don't judge my teddy bear," she started, "It's the only thing I have from my childhood. When I decided to leave my mom's home it was the only thing I brought with me." I stared at the teddy bear.

"I remember that teddy bear. You've literally had that bear since you were six. It was always on your dresser in your room when I used to come over. After all these years it still looks new." She stood up.

"I consider it my guardian angel. It's actually been around more than you. Through all the drug use, the overuse of alcohol, the battling the voices in my head, the teddy bear has always been there. I can't believe I've never given it a name. And disregard any of those words I said. I would have only meant them if you were dead. Fuck you and everything you stand for, now that I know you're alive." I burst out laughing.

"Well, thank you for the kind words. What's for breakfast? Have you cooked?" Well, that's a dumb question, considering I know she's been sitting in front of my door all night and probably hasn't had any sleep.

"Marcus, when are we going to have the talk we've been avoiding? The talk where we put all our secrets on the table and leave them there. That talk is overdue and you know it." I told her a secret and she didn't believe me. "Holy shit, I just realized something. Is Camille the woman that turned Tiffany to the other side?"

"Shit."

"Yes, you told me Tiffany was gay. Holy shit again, you were kissing her! What kind of freaky shit do you have going on?" I put my hand on my forehead and closed my eyes. "Marcus, that whole scene is making sense. My memory works weird. Things don't start making sense until days and weeks later."

"Christina, it's a very long story that you won't understand. I'm having a hard time understanding it. It's quite complicated. I could tell you the entire story and end up telling it completely wrong. I guess it depends on who's telling you the story."

"So, she likes you and Tiffany?" she asked.

"Did you miss the part where I said it's a long and complicated story?" She shook her head in disgust and walked away. "Hey, what pills do you have for depression?" She stopped and turned around. Her face is showing no emotion.

"Marcus, if you really needed pills for depression, I wouldn't give them to you. If I knew then what I know now, I would have stayed on drugs. At least I was in a different, happier world, even if it was all in my head. The side effects of all these pills aren't worth it. I don't know exactly what you're going through, but my advice to you is to figure it out sober or die trying. Prescription pills will do more damage than good, especially for someone with a mind like yours. I will not allow you to go down that path. Thank me later." She walked into her room and closed the door.

"Thanks for nothing," I hollered. What if I'm tired of trying to figure things out? What if trying to figure things out have got me nowhere? Sometimes the psych ward doesn't seem so bad. Put me in a padded room, load me up on pills and let me live inside my head. She may be able to stop me from getting pills, but she can't stop me from getting liquor. I've just realized that I've been more open to being in a psych ward.

"And your mom went into a coma from drinking too much liquor at once," she hollered from her room. "I went to the hospital to find out for myself since you don't believe in telling me anything important." Wow, I didn't even know that, or cared to find out. Maybe that's my sign to not go to the liquor store. With how much liquor I've consumed at once, I should have been in a coma a long time ago. Why couldn't Mom have my type of luck? What was she using the liquor to escape from that final time?

I've received a text message from Tiffany saying her and Camille want to meet up with me. I'll pass on that offer. I'm not ready to start seeing them as a couple yet. Essentially, Tiffany is getting lied to by the both of us. Why am I the only one suffering? Now Tiffany is calling me. I guess I took too long to text her back.

"Yes," I kindly answered.

"Did you receive my text?" she anxiously asked.

"I did, but didn't know I was obligated to text you back."

"What's your problem this morning?" I almost said something harsh. Anger is not going to change anything, and I must remember that she has my child in her stomach. Everything is my problem. This entire situation is my problem, though I may be the cause of some of it. At least I've tried to make things right. My attempts have been a total failure.

"There's no problem, I'm just trying to enjoy my day. I don't think meeting up with the two of you will make my day enjoyable. Anything we need to discuss we can discuss right now." She sighed.

"Marcus, you're being petty and problematic for no reason. Are you going to be this way through this entire process?" I should hang up now. Though we're not together I still feel we shouldn't be arguing. I feel a huge argument coming. Why am I thinking about her well-being? She's not thinking about mine. Oh yeah, because she's carrying my seed. Another priority that puts me at a disadvantage.

"Fine, we can meet up. Text me when and where and I'll meet the two of you there." I ended the call. Now I have to find something to wear. Grey sweatpants and a t-shirt will be fine. I should ask Christina to come with me, but don't want to bring her into the unknown. I don't even know what we're meeting up for. This would be a perfect time for me to run away. This child has changed everything.

They really want to meet at Barnes and Noble, me and Tiffany's favorite place. The irony of this, and I'm the one being problematic? I'm headed to our favorite place to bond, there's no point in me complaining though I really want to. Great, "Break Up To Make Up" by The Stylistics just came on. I love this song. My mom used to play it all the time when I was a child. "Break-up to make-up, that's all we do, first you love me, then you hate me, that's a game for fools." My singing is horrible.

I've become agitated now that I'm in Barnes and Noble. I feel like I'm here for all the wrong reasons. I see Camille and Tiffany sitting at a table. I should turn around and walk away. The two women I love are sitting together at a table being in love with each other. "What is it you two want to talk about?" I asked as I approached the table. I sat down.

"We need to talk," Camille said.

"Tell me something I don't know." They both shook their heads. "Why are you shaking your heads? I'm making it obvious I don't want to be here. Any conversation needed could have been conducted on the phone." Tiffany took a deep breath.

"You know what? I can't do this." Tiffany stood up. "I've done everything completely wrong. Marcus, we took time apart but I didn't take time to heal." She turned towards Camille. "I've been unfair to you. Do I love you? Yes. Do I enjoy feeling your lips on my body? Absolutely. I don't think it's fair to be with you when I haven't completely pushed Marcus away, which will be much harder now that we have a child together."

"I'm confused," I started, "You mean to tell me we couldn't have had this conversation on the phone? I'm not sure how I'm needed for this conversation now that I think about it."

"Well," Camille started, "We'd brought you here for a different reason." I turned my glance towards Camille. "We wanted Tiffany to have the baby and we become a family without you being involved." I gasped. I think I'm losing my breath. I need to relax. I must breathe my way through this. "I guess someone had a change of heart when we arrived. I wish the change of heart would have occurred earlier."

"Tiffany, you're really considering me not being in my child's life? Why are you trying to make it seem like I'm some type of animal?" Tears are starting to form in Tiffany's eyes. I want to get loud in this Barnes and Noble but must stay conscious of the fact my child is in her stomach. Camille looks as if she's annoyed, and though I hate her at the moment, I totally understand where she's coming from.

"I don't know what I want," Tiffany cried out. "I just need to be away from everyone to get my thoughts together. I want the truth, whatever that may consist of. I thought the truth consists of loyalty, peace and happiness, but realized I had all of that and somehow ruined it." She took a deep breath. "I'm going somewhere to paint for the rest of the day. Please don't call me. I'll find my way back home when I'm tired of painting." She walked away.

"I assume she's going to use an Uber to get around," Camille said. I turned towards Camille. If I was ever going to choke someone to death, right now would be the moment. I'll sit down and do my time. I've experienced jail, prison can't be much worse.

"Camille, have you lost your mind?" I lowly asked, not hiding the anger in my voice. "You really attempted to remove me out my child's life? Bitch, are you crazy?"

"Well, that's the first time you've ever used that word towards me. I guess this is the time I finally get to see the angry side of Marcus." There's no fear in her voice. I guess she's smart enough to know I'm not going to do anything crazy to her while in here. "It wasn't my idea to remove you from the child's life. What was I supposed to say? She is my girlfriend." I've been wanting to scream a lot lately. "I should have stayed in California."

"Camille, who do you love more? Tiffany or me?"

"You, of course. What type of question is that?" I buried my face into my hands. "Marcus, through all of this, please know my heart will always be with you. Yes, I have feelings for Tiffany and her uniqueness, but if it was possible for you and me to run away to another state and start over, I'd do it instantly." I lifted my head.

"Tell me something, since you don't even like women, how did you fall for Tiffany? It's really mindboggling to me. I can't figure it out and I've tried looking at it from all angles."

"Tiffany is the woman I aspire to be. Tiffany is the woman I thought didn't exist. To be honest, I have a hard time figuring out what made you cheat when you had such a perfect woman. All the categories of a good woman she checks off. It's a different ballgame when you're trying to figure things out from the outside. Now that I actually see how she acts and the type of person she is, it sends a bunch of different thoughts into my head."

"Thoughts like what?" She has my full attention now.

"I feel guilty. I feel like I ruined something really good, though that wasn't my intentions. It seems like the two of you are fit for each other. Then I tell myself we're fit for each other, but not like the two of you are. Part of me says to let go of it all. The other part reminds me that the damage has been done. You and Tiffany will never be the same again. Marcus, I just want to be happy."

"I think that's what everyone in life wants." I touched her hand. "If only life provided us with a handbook on how to obtain it." I lifted her hand and kissed it. It seems like whatever direction I take, I end up back in the same spot, the spot of confusion. How did this situation become so complicated?

"Will any of us ever obtain it?" Camille asked. The first response that came to my head isn't the response I should say aloud. Happiness seems to be possible, I just believe we all take the wrong route to obtain it, and when we do obtain it, we somehow find a way to ruin it. It's almost like we're more comfortable with dysfunction. Happiness is too peaceful.

"I don't know," I replied. "I don't know."

****

Tiffany hasn't been home in two days according to Camille. She's at home freaking out while I'm coming to the realization that you reap what you sow. All those times I went missing for various reasons are now happening to me. It's worse because she's carrying my child. I'm not worried though. Worrying never helps the situation.

My job let me know I'm fired, which is fine. I've missed so many days that I'm shocked it didn't happen sooner. Maybe when I get my life in order I'll start back working. Maybe my life will never be organized again. Maybe the organized life wasn't real. Maybe a life of chaos is the reality.

"Marcus, may you please tell Julie to shut up," Christina demanded as she walked into my room. She's been holding her teddy bear more often like it's really her guardian angel.

"Julie, shut up." I meanly said. She walked over, hugged me, and kissed me on the cheek.

"Thank you," she smiled. "I think there's another level of craziness I haven't reached. I've been having these horrible dreams."

"Do you need me to start back sleeping beside you?" She squeezed her teddy bear.

"No, because you represent hope. When you're lying by me I start believing that everything will be alright. My friends hate when you're sleeping next to me. They don't talk to me as often. Bryan says it's not possible for you to sleep by me every day and he's right. He says you'll eventually leave and it will just be me, him, Julie, Zach, Mariah, Gilbert, and Cindy, bonding like we always do. He says to not get comfortable with you because it's not everlasting."

"Tell Bryan I said fuck him and everything he believes in." She smiled and nodded her head. "After my child, you're the next person on my list of importance. You understand me better than most, and may understand me more than myself if I opened up to you, which is why I won't. I trust you with my life and truly believe you wouldn't let anything harmful happen to me, if it's in your control."

"Well, after my teddy bear, you're next on my list of importance." I nodded my head and smiled. "I have to go take my medicine, or death pills, depending on how you look at it." She walked out of my room. I just figured out the change with Christina. It seems like she's a younger age all of a sudden.

I want to call Tiffany but am sure she has her phone powered off. I know where she's at. She's at her mom's home. That's where she goes to get away. Her mom cares about her enough that she will lie and say she's not there. Her dad lives there too, but her mom runs the show, so I just say it's her mom's home, though her dad makes the most money. Tiffany was blessed to have both parents in the house to raise her.

I just received a text message from Camille asking for me to come over. I want Camille to go away, just so Tiffany and I can try to figure things out. It's hard for Tiffany to see things clearly with her around. If it was my final decision I'd used the rest of my bank account money to send Camille back to California. Things have changed now that I have a child on the way. Now I must be a better example.

"Marcus, what are we doing?" She got off me and grabbed a towel. So much for me being a better example. I don't remember the last time we had sex, but we just made up for it in their room. The world needs to end. I'm tired of everything. "How are we having sex when we're supposed to be worrying about Tiffany?" I stared at the ceiling.

"Maybe we're both insane and are just lying to ourselves," I replied. "Maybe we really don't love her like we say we do. Maybe we tell ourselves whatever sounds good just to make it through the day. Maybe neither of us are meant to be with her. We both may know it deep down inside. That fact has us battling each other, trying to avoid the inevitable."

"Marcus, where do these odd thoughts come from?"

"Depression," I quickly replied and got out the bed. What am I doing here? How does a person lose himself so quickly? I used to have morals, what happened to them? I'm not wishing bad on myself, but if I knew then what I know now, I wish I would have died in that car accident. Things have been steadily going downhill and I don't know how to reverse it.

"When did you start suffering from depression?" Camille asked as she put her clothes on. I don't know why, but looking at her now disgusts me. Maybe I'm just disgusted with myself and don't know how to deal with it. I don't know, my thoughts are everywhere. I just want to sit in a corner and cry. I've lost control over myself when I've been known as a disciplined person for so long. Chemically, something has changed inside of me.

"Maybe I've been depressed for years and haven't realized it. Maybe I've been able to block it out. I believe I've had my life structured to not have to think about it. The structures have now collapsed and I'm face to face with all my problems."

"Are you blaming me for that structure breakdown?" she asked. I nodded my head. Maybe the depression didn't start until I met her. Or maybe she was the sign from God to make me realize I've been depressed. I can admit I don't know anything anymore and don't know how to go about searching for answers. "Marcus, I think you're looking for someone to blame." I started putting on my clothes. "At the end of the day, I believe you're just not happy because you've lost control of everything. You've become a different person since you've seemed to lose your grip over this situation."

"Maybe you enjoy having control over me. Maybe you purposely tried to loosen my grip because you hated seeing me poised. You used love to blind me." She shook her head.

"Marcus, all I've ever wanted was to be loved, that's it, it's really that simple. There is no side motive when you're genuinely searching for love. I know I say I live in the moment, but there's replays of my past creeping close behind. It's a battle trying not to fall back into that mode of giving up. When I give up I accept that my past is going to be my future. I'm never going to be loved. All my dad's words were true. My mom cursed me and I will curse everyone who comes into my path on an emotional level, though it's the farthest from my intentions."

"You should go see your parents and get closure over your past," I said. She threw her hands up, grabbed her purse, and pulled out her wallet. She pulled out a card and handed it to me. It's her old identification card, and she's clearly a man, that actually looks nothing like how she looks now. He has a few of her features, but overall, the doctor did a great job in changing her.

"How can I go back to my parents for closure when that is the person they remember?" This is the closure I've needed but desperately tried to avoid. I've always had in a small place in my mind that this was all a joke. I know I've said I accepted if she was a man in the past, and it hasn't even been brought up during recent arguments, but I said it, keeping this slight hope in the back of my mind that it would all be a joke. The joke is over. The reality is here and I don't know how to feel about it.

"I don't know what to say." I handed her the card back. She really used to be Cornell. It hasn't all been a lie. I'd even told myself I liked her because her mind was crazy enough to create this story in her head, and repeat it till the point it would become her reality. I was admitting I liked her craziness. The entire time it's been me that's been crazy. It's been me that's been creating the story in my head.
"I guess I will be scarred forever." She sat on the bed. I will

continue to stand. I feel like this is the part when I'm supposed to have a mental breakdown. I'm supposed to replay in my head that she's been a man the entire time. I don't know what a mental breakdown consists of, but I do know I'm still standing here, in the moment, without any blackouts or outbursts.

"I'm going to leave now," I slowly said. Everything feels like it's moving in slow motion. Before now, life had seemed to be moving quickly. Now it seems like life is purposely slowing down, begging for me to inhale this moment. It's begging for me to accept this reality.

"Please, take this diary entry I wrote today." She picked up her tablet and handed it to me. I don't want to read it. Something is telling me to throw the tablet on the floor. I don't want to attach myself to any more of her words. I want to detach myself as much as possible. What am I doing here?

I closed the door and turned on the car. I need a session of meditation ASAP. My thoughts are everywhere and they're not happy thoughts. I banged my head on the steering wheel. The anger I'm feeling right now is unexplainable. I banged my head on the steering wheel again. After seeing what she showed, I'm not sure who I'm more upset with, her or myself. I banged my head on the steering wheel again. The feelings are still there. I'd think after seeing that identification card the feelings would quickly leave, which means I don't know myself like I thought I did. I banged my head on the steering wheel again. I just want to forget about everything.

I want to be with my mom. I don't want to commit suicide, I feel that's the easy way out, but I do want to be with my mom. I need comfort. I need my head rubbed and assurance that everything is going to be alright. I feel empty. Liquor won't fill this emptiness, which says a lot because I feel like liquor will cure anything. Dealing with situations used to not be a problem for me. I felt every problem would help me grow. I think I've finally met my match.

Camille just knocked on my car window. I didn't see her come outside. I must have really been zoned into my own world. I let down my window. "Marcus, I love you," she sincerely stated. The truth has been revealed. I know all the facts now. What am I supposed to say to her? Are the feelings still there? Yes. I want the burning desire to leave, but what if it doesn't? What if the feeling isn't meant to leave? Am I supposed to be this way?

"I'll talk to you soon," I replied.

"Marcus, say it back. Say that you love me." I turned away. I want to let up the window and drive away but feel stuck. "Marcus, don't look away! Tell me our bond is everlasting." I let up my window. I can't do it. I can't continue to let this go on. She's banging her hand on the window. I will not let the window back down. This will be the last time I ever speak to Camille, I swear on my life. If it's not then God can take my life away for lying. With all the lying I've been doing, he should have killed me a long time ago.

"What are you doing?" I asked Christina as I walked into the house. She's lying on the tile floor, in front of the door, looking at the ceiling. She has an opened tablet next to her, which makes me assume she's been writing.

"Marcus, read this and tell me if I'm crazy." She leaned up, handed me the tablet and laid back down. I thought we'd come to a conclusion about her craziness. Maybe her hearing the words will bring some peace into her life. If that's the case then she will never have any peace. I will never say those words out loud, though I've heard her call herself crazy.

Dear Diary,

I was done with it all. I was done letting the voices control me to an extent. I was done letting the drugs and liquor (that I've been hiding from Marcus) control me. As soon as I noticed Marcus becoming sober is when I decided to relapse. If I was in a twelve-step program, I'd say I was on step eleven. Now I'm back at step one. I'm now going through all the emotions and damaging thoughts I'd moved on from. Add that to my current emotions and damaging thoughts I'm experiencing and you officially have a……I don't know what to call me. How did I allow myself to get back to this point? What in my brain thought this would be a good idea? I hate myself. I want to die now. I think I'm in line for the cycle of bullshit. I'm going to get better, realize I'm getting better, then relapse and do it all over again. If this is the case then what's the point in trying? Why not stay at step one? Maybe trying to get better is pointless. Maybe I'm supposed to be this way. Maybe I've been running from what's meant to be. Maybe I'm supposed to be this damaged person and there's some greater lesson I'm not paying attention to. I guess I'll go pop me a few pills now.

Christina

"Christina, are you high right now?" I closed the tablet.

"High as a kite," she quickly responded. "And please don't ask me what pills I'm on at the moment. They have me feeling amazing."

"Why did you get back on drugs? Why didn't you tell me?"

"Marcus, may we talk about this after my high goes away? I'm really feeling amazing right now." I walked past her. I'm really mad at her right now, but know that expressing my anger won't help anything. I will never understand her thought process. I couldn't recognize her getting better, but if she truly was, why mess it up? Maybe everything isn't meant for me to understand. Matter of fact, I'm going to turn around and leave. I need to be around a different energy.

I closed my car door. Camille's tablet is next to me. My gut is telling me not to read it. What could she possibly have written that I don't know about? I don't want to know anything else about her. I want to be away from everything. I want to find a place where I can sit and be depressed for the rest of my life. I already know I'll never be the same mentally. I'm accepting that reality now. I opened her tablet.

Dear Life,

I have so many words, but don't know where to start. All I want is for someone that knows my secret to ask am I happy. It's a simple question. Does no one think about this? No one ever asks about the surgery for the change, which was the most painful experience ever, and will forever be painful for me. No one asks do I actually feel like a woman now. No one asks do I regret my decision in hindsight. Would it have been easier to stay a man and just date men? Was it a bad idea to want to become my mom? No one seems to care about my emotional well-being. Only a few people know, but none ever ask any of these questions. Did I make the best decision or worst mistake ever? Would I do it all again? Was it worth it? What were those sessions like with my psychiatrist before going through with the surgery? Do I ever get depressed and miss how things used to be? What type of medications am I taking? Just some questions I ask myself but never answer.

Camille

I walked in and closed the door. I'm here, uninvited, but he will understand. I haven't been here in a while and felt awkward trying to call and make an appointment. He's sitting with a woman who he seems to be in a deep conversation with. Maybe that's why they didn't hear the door open.

"I don't know how to let go," the woman started. "It's a complicated situation. When I was a child I woke up to seeing my dad and aunt having sex on the floor. I was five years old and it's been in my memory ever since. The thought has haunted me. It's changed my perspective on life."

"Elaborate," the psychiatrist said.

"I've had a sense of feeling like no one is worthy and no one is faithful. I saw this with my own eyes at the age of five. What is going on here? What is my family doing right now? I'm now older and have a better way of understanding things, but it still makes no sense. My boyfriend experienced the same situation, now we feel like we're meant to be together, though it's clear we're not compatible. We're just damaged people maneuvering our way through life."

"So, what exactly is your problem?"

"Everything is my problem. My thoughts are distorted. I tend to tell myself that maybe my boyfriend is the right one. Maybe

I'm the problem. My boyfriend is an interesting case. He hates his mom for sleeping with his uncle. Neither of us have approached our parents about it. We're both just kind of dealing with it together."

"How do you deal with it?" he asked. She took a deep breath. "Do you need a glass of water?" She shook her head.

"We don't deal with it. We hold each other a lot and enjoy the exchange of negative energy. There's always silence in the air but we feel like we can hear each other talking. He doesn't have to tell me. I know he hates his mom. I know he'll never truly love a woman. The heartbreak has happened before the relationship is official."

"Is your perspective the same?"

"No," she quickly replied. "I'm damaged, but there's a tiny dot of hope I try to keep. I try to believe in the fairytale. I try to believe there's a light at the end of the tunnel, though I feel I'll never get there. It's still good to strive for it, right? I'm a horribly optimistic person."

"So, you're an optimist and your boyfriend is a pessimist?" She looked down at the ground.

"He thinks all women are bitches. He calls me a bitch a lot and screams he hates me. He says my pussy feels different when I've clearly had sex with no one else. He lashes out at me a lot, physically and verbally. I don't think it's me he's really lashing out on. I really think it's his mother. When I pack my bags to leave, he sits in a corner and cries. My soul melts each time because I think I understand his pain."

"His pain causes you to stay?"

"I think we have the same pain, but go about handling it differently. I'm more bottled up with my pain. I sometimes feel that I should be acting like him. I can sit around my dad with a heart full of hate and still have a full conversation with him. I see the filth in his eyes but see the love in my mom's eyes. She has no clue what her husband did. My aunt comes around like everything is great. If I had to guess I'd say they're still having sex. It seems obvious in my eyes, but maybe because I already know what they've done."

"Do you want to explain the pain you're feeling?" I quietly opened the door and walked out. It's obvious I won't be seeing him anytime soon. I now feel horrible for standing there and listening to their conversation. It was none of my business but will admit the conversation pulled me in. You never know what someone is going through on the inside.

Now that I'm in the car, I want to analyze the pain I'm experiencing. Thanks a lot lady. I rather hide the pain, though I feel like the scars will eventually get too deep. Things have changed too drastically to go back to normal. I flirted with living life on the edge, now wishing I would have walked off the cliff. I no longer recognize anything in my life. Every action I've made in the past year seems like the wrong one. Oh well, I just have to deal with it. Camille just texted me. I'm going to ignore her like I promised I would.

I pulled up to their home. I'm not going to question myself. I'm here, so I may as well deal with it. If I suddenly die, I'll have no one to blame. That's the deal I made with God and she has me breaking it. Why can't I loosen from her tight grip? It seems like the harder I pull away, the tighter the grip becomes. It's quite depressing.

"Another transgender got killed today." She pulled out a pack of cigarettes from her purse. I closed the front door, walked over, and stood by the couch. "Before you start to judge me, know that I don't smoke cigarettes. These are my vice when I'm stressing extremely hard." She put the cigarette in her mouth and pulled out her lighter.

"Why am I here?" I asked. "What was the point in calling me? I made a vow to never speak to you again. This is the first time I've come back but can say to myself I'm truly unhappy to be here. I'm over this entire situation. At least that's what I tell myself."

"Marcus, may you stop thinking about yourself for a minute? Did you hear what I said? Another transgender was killed today.

That's the eighth murder of that kind for the year. It scares me, it makes me feel like I'm alone in this world."

"Camille, we're all alone in this world. It just isn't you." I want to sit down but don't want to get comfortable here. I've realized that I've become comfortable with discomfort. At that point is where my life started to change for the worse. I wish it wouldn't have taken me so long to realize this.

"Marcus, I don't think you understand. It may not be possible for you to understand. What if someone finds out about me and attempts to kill me? How is that fair? You can't kill me because of MY choice to have a lifestyle change. It's MY choice."

"Camille, no one is going to kill you," I bluntly replied. "May I leave now? You're here being paranoid for no reason."

"How can you be so sure? This is a sick world we live in. We have a bunch of lunatics running around acting like they're God and have the right to choose who lives and dies. When I look at life from that perspective it makes me wonder if there really is a God. Why give lunatics so much power?"

"Camille, get some sleep. You're overthinking for no reason. Stop watching the news. We tend to think a lot of things into existence. The thoughts usually come from what we're looking at and subconsciously planting into our minds. You're going to be fine." I started for the front door.

"Marcus, please sit here with me for a few hours. I don't want to be alone, I'm scared. No, I don't want any sex. I just want someone in my presence who gives me a sense of security."

"That's what Tiffany is for. I know she's at work, but that's not my problem. We all can't have everything we want. I'm done with this game. I'm done with this circle of confusion. I'm done with it all. I'm tired of repeating myself so I'm breaking the cycle and sticking to my word."

"All I ever wanted was to be happy and not feel alone," she sadly stated. "I wanted the hole in my heart to be filled. I wanted to no longer feel like an outcast. I've just wanted to feel accepted."

"Well, I hope you received what you've been searching for." I opened the door and walked out. This is my last time saying this is the last time, though my heart is aching while saying it.

"Marcus, please don't leave me!" I'm already outside and refuse to turn around. I'm having the urge to run away again but know I can't. This unexpected child has changed everything. I wish my mom was here to see this. She always wanted a grandchild. I just texted Christina, telling her to meet me at the beach. The beach is the closest thing to running away that I will get to experience.

"Have you accepted it?" Christina asked.

"Have I accepted what?"

"Your mom's death. Let me rephrase that. How do you cope with your mom being dead? I'm not sure if you can ever accept it. You've already admitted to her death changing you." I took a deep breath. She is the first person to ask me this question. I really don't have an answer. I haven't put much thought into it. I could tell her about how I tried to literally drink myself to death, but I'll refrain.

"I don't think I cope with it at all. I just go through the motions. Thinking about her saddens me, so I try not to think about her. I really can't explain it. I'm not numb to it like I said I was, I just don't want to give any feelings to it. Any feelings to it won't change the fact she's gone. I guess I can just hope that she's looking down on me from heaven. It's so peaceful being out here at the beach."

"I wish someone would have brought me here earlier. I haven't felt this type of relaxation in a long time. It's something about the sound of the water and waves that does something to me. It's almost like I'm away from life." She moved closer to me. She's right, there's no better feeling than looking at the water while sitting on the sand. I never want to leave.

"Christina, do you ever wish you could start over?" She looks like she's in deep thought. I would love to dive inside her brain to see what her thoughts are daily. I may be shocked at what I find out, but I'd still like to know.

"You want to start over?" she asked. "Well, fuck it, we're starting over then. Let's go home and pack our bags. Where are we going? Don't answer that. We can figure it out once we get on the road. Let's run away from our demons. If they catch us then we'll continue to run."

"I can't leave. I have a child on the way. I must be in my child's life, there's no alternative. I will never do my child the way my father did me." She gently touched my shoulder. Being at the beach has allowed me to forgive Christina for relapsing. We will discuss it one day, but no day soon. I'm learning that you have to let some people live.

"Well then, we'll stay here on our never-ending search for happiness. Will we find it? Probably not, but can try to. I don't know how we'll go about finding it. We've obviously been going about it the wrong way. We may not find it, but we'll figure something out. We always do." I nodded my head in agreement. I hope she's right.

****

Wow, we've made it. Through all the obstacles, here I am, standing in front of this church in my black tuxedo, watching each specific friend and family member walk down the aisle. If it was up to me this would have been a much smaller wedding, but Tiffany gets what she wants, and I'm not going to complain about it. I'm going to inhale the air and enjoy the moment. The moment may not be as genuine as I envisioned it would be, but at least it's here.

It's amazing how much has changed in the past year. My mom has died, my dad is back into my life, Tiffany and I have cheated on each other with the same person, and my life has turned into a cycle of lies. With all of that, I still stand here waiting to officially get married. No, Tiffany and I don't love each other like we once did, but the outside world will never know that. Yes, we are doing this for our child, and yes, my ulterior motive is knowing that the family perception to the outside world is a great look, and I care about perception.

Everyone who's in the wedding seems so happy. My dad's smile is from ear to ear, like he's been in my life the entire time and is happy to see me finally make it to this point. Tiffany's mom's face is expressing happiness, only because she doesn't know the entire story. She knows Tiffany and I disagree at times and Tiffany runs there to get away, but if she had any real idea, I'm sure she wouldn't have any reason to smile. She may attempt to kill me, and I wouldn't stop her.

Christina decided to be in the wedding. She's the most loyal person I'll ever have in my life. She should be the person I'm marrying. I know we really care for each other. Deep flaws have been exposed and we didn't run away. I'm upset she never accepted my 800 dollars. Today is my wedding so I'll think about that later.

Annoyance has overcome my body now that my eyes have reached Camille's. I argued against this until the very last second. How are we going to allow the person who's responsible for all our pain to be in our wedding? I understand our feelings are very high for her---- no, I take that back. My feelings for her are dead. My feelings were manipulated and I don't accept that. Am I lying to myself? Of course I am, but before committing to this wedding, I made a promise to fight my urges. I have to be a good example. We still haven't spoken since that day. Through all the wedding rehearsals we'd ignore each other. I've made it known to Tiffany that I don't like her.

Though I hate her, Camille has a trait that a lot of people lack, and that's loyalty. She never told Tiffany, which is quite shocking, considering everything we've been through. Tiffany has been in the dark the entire time. She still blames herself for everything. If Camille and I were on speaking terms, I'd thank her for not completely ruining my life.

Tiffany has reached me and looks beautiful. Her stomach is growing. She's not fat yet, but it's clearly noticeable she's pregnant. I wanted this wedding to happen while she was still small enough to avoid any self-esteem issues. We turned towards the pastor.

"Today, we have two beautiful souls coming together," the pastor started. "They're taking the vow that seems so rare today, the vow to be together forever through the highs and lows, through thick and thin." The audience clapped. I haven't been to a wedding before, but I'm not sure if this is the appropriate time to clap. "Now, before we start, is there anyone who disagrees with this marriage happening?"

"I do," Camille said. She stepped up and grabbed the microphone. "I have something to say." She turned to Tiffany. "I've been holding in a lot of secrets." Oh shit.

www.ingramcontent.com/pod-product-compliance
Lightning Source LLC
Chambersburg PA
CBHW061431040426
42450CB00007B/994